Echoes of the Past
Sherwood, Oregon
(503) 625-ECHO

COLLECTOR'S
ENCYCLOPEDIA OF

Sascha Brastoff

IDENTIFICATION & VALUES

Steve Conti
A. DeWayne Bethany
Bill Seay

COLLECTOR BOOKS
A Division of Schroeder Publishing Co., Inc.

The current values in this book should be used only as a guide. They are not intended to set prices, which vary from one section of the country to another. Auction prices as well as dealer prices vary greatly and are affected by condition as well as demand. Neither the Authors nor the Publisher assumes responsibility for any losses that might be incurred as a result of consulting this guide.

———•+——   ——•+——

Searching For A Publisher?

We are always looking for knowledgeable people considered to be experts within their fields. If you feel there is a real need for a book on your collectible subject and have a large comprehensive collection, contact Collector Books.

———•+——   ——•+——

We would love to hear from other collectors about their personal collections, questions on unusual pieces or just comments on our book!

If you wish to write the authors, or would like more information regarding a particular Sascha item, you may reach us at the address below. Please send a S.A.S.E. for the return shipments.

"More Gold!"
256 South Robertson Blvd.
Suite 109
Beverly Hills, CA 90211

———•+——   ——•+——

On the Cover:
"Pea Fowl," 23" welded metal rod sculpture, $2,500.00 estate (see page 153).
"Faun Mask," 13", style M31, $750.00 (see page 255).
"Star Steed," 12" plate, given to Bill Seay by Sascha; then by Bill to Steve Conti. NPA.
"Piranha," 16"x20" oil and gesso, $1,950.00 estate (see page 266).

Cover Design: Beth Summers
Book Design: Beth Ray
Edited By: Lisa Stroup

Additional copies of this book may be ordered from:

A. DeWayne Bethany
256 South Robertson Blvd. Suite 109
Beverly Hills, CA 90211

or

COLLECTOR BOOKS
P.O. Box 3009
Paducah, Kentucky 42002-3009

@$24.95. Add $2.00 for postage and handling.

❧ Contents ❧

✎ Dedication ✎

Mrs. Evelyn Leftofsky (Sascha's sister) and her husband.

The authors would like to dedicate this book to Sascha Brastoff's beloved sister, Mrs. Evelyn Leftofsky, whose lifelong love, encouragement, and belief in his talent were cherished by Sascha until his passing.

We would also like to dedicate this book to Sascha's friend, Filomena Bruno, whose warmth, caring, sensitivity, and non-stop humor kept Sascha smiling through the good times and bad.

Filomena Bruno.

We are most appreciative for all of their help with this project.

❦ *Acknowledgments* ❦

The authors wish to extend a warm and heartfelt thank you to the following individuals or organizations whose love, support, and talent contributed to the production of this book.

Joseph Abbamont
Horace L. Allfrey
Verna M. Allfrey
the staff of the Antique Guild
Rogel Aragon
Claudy J. Bethany
Dan Earl Bethany
Laura L. Bethany
Nicky Blair
Kozell & Sally Cannon Boren
David Byrnes
Henry Carasas
James Paul Carr
Terry Clifford
the staff of Colortek
The Conti Family
Marilyn Contreras
Harold Cunningham
Richard Victor David
Jerry Deakin
Mr. & Mrs. Roy W. Dodson Jr.
Diane Eberly
Daniel E. Fast, M.D.

April Franklin
Leo Freeman
Robert Grady Golden
Arthur Green
Al Guarino
Fred Guenthart
Russell E. Harris
Harold W. Hogan
Mary Horst
Gordon Irvine
Pamela Johnston
Ula Johnson
David Kennedy
Gene Kincaid
Eugene Maiden
dearest Marusja
Jerry McKenna
Joquin Borge Mediavilla
Mitz Murakami
Robert T. Neff
Tim Neil
Don Norwine
Kitty Pease

William Perry, Ph.D.
The Plunkett Family
Jamie Robinson
The Ruiz Family
Ann Rutherford
Diane & Robert Schumacher
Edith Seay
J.E. Seay
Lyn & Ed Sherer
James H. Shumaker, M.D.
Charles Smiley Jr.
Duncan Smith
Ken Stalcup
Sebastian Stevens
Elizabeth Von Arnswaldt
Eva F. Webb
Payton R. Webb
The Wenzel Family
Dick Wimer
Mas Yamashita
Don Zoutte

...and a very special thank you to Mrs. Winthrop B. Rockefeller, photographer Rick Flynn, Zachary Charles Greenberg and our editor Lisa Stroup & the entire Collector Books team!

Editor's Note: "Sascha produced custom artistic erotica exclusively for some very famous, wealthy, and influential people. These items, referred to as 'back door pieces,' were never offered for sale to the general public and were often unsigned. They are most highly prized by today's sophisticated collectors and, due to their adult themes, were not pictorially represented in this book."

❧ *About The Authors* ❧

A. DeWayne Bethany first met Sascha when Bethany owned an antique shop in Venice, California. It was the height of the Beat Generation — 1951. Sascha would stop by to browse almost every Friday; the early start of a long weekend. He would limit his buying to curious items: tribal figures, Indian masks, things from the four corners of the world. Many influenced his pottery designs and decoration. Like most creative types of the day, Dee and Sascha formed a bond and began to socialize together. They remained close friends until Sascha's passing in 1993.

Bill Seay met Sascha when he applied for a staff position as an artist at the new Brastoff factory (late 1952). Bill had been an actor since he was only six months old and appeared in such classics as *Topaze* with John Barrymore and *The Unknown* with Joan Crawford. Seay's father was a successful Los Angeles artist and Bill an accomplished painter in his own right. Bill worked with Sascha from 1952 to 1959, after which he was a commissioned portrait artist for stars like Judy Garland, Joan Crawford, and George Reeves. It was Bill's continual friendship, humor, and encouragement that saw Sascha through good times and bad, be it a new business venture or a simple Thursday night card game. They were close to the end. Currently Bill uses his talents in the antiques and decorating trade in Los Angeles.

Steve Conti worked as a writer/producer of television and film promotion for five years until starting a business in twentieth century decorative arts. He currently plans to independently produce the film version of the Brastoff biography, for release in 1996.

Seay, Conti, and Bethany with an original silk watercolor by Sascha.

⌇ *Foreword* ⌇

JEANNETTE E. ROCKEFELLER

Jeannette Edris Rockefeller.

May 9, 1994

U.S. Mail Overnight

Mr. Steve Conti

Dear Mr. Conti:

I first met Sascha Brastoff at the home of my then fiancé, Win Rockefeller; they had been friends for years and I became his friend as well. We became very close as the years went by, he was always there when I needed him. When my father was terminally ill, Sascha came to stay with me to hold my hand. When I was in the hospital with back problems he would visit and tell hilariously funny stories to cheer me.

Although Sascha was best known for his work in ceramics, he was in truth a multitalented artist. He was a fine painter, a sculptor whose beautiful cross can be seen in the church of St. Augustine-by-the-Sea. Sascha taught me to enamel and there is a huge wonderful mural at Winrock Farms and I have some enamel paintings that are unique. He was a jeweler of renown creating one of a kind rings, pins, earrings of gold and pearls and precious stones. I have examples of all of his work and one ring in particular I wear every day, a beautiful golden dome. When I put it on in the morning, I think of our loving friendship. I will miss him always.

Jeannette Rockefeller

7

❧ *Preface* ❧

Bill Seay: Sascha was a friend and confidante of over 42 years. We became fast friends from the start as we both had ties to the movie industry. I had been under contract to M.G.M., Warner Bros., and Samuel Goldwyn as a child actor. I grew up with Judy Garland, Mickey Rooney and Bonita Granville. Sascha had been under contract to 20th Century Fox as an actor and costume designer. From the start, I knew Sascha was a true undiscovered artistic genius and sculptor of the twentieth century. He was outstanding in whatever medium he decided to pursue. While working with Sascha for seven years in his Olympic Boulevard factory, I was dazzled by his designs for pottery and china. He was a great dancer and an actor-mimic. He kept me laughing constantly with his ribald stories of Hollywood and its stars which he had as clients down through the years. When Sascha found out I was doing great candid shots around the factory, he bought me all the camera equipment I needed to do his catalogues for two years. I almost hated to collect my salary as it was a real joy working for him. After seven years, I finally left Sascha to do portrait photography. We remained close friends until his death. I miss him still.

A. DeWayne Bethany: I wish I had known some day I would help write a book about Sascha Brastoff and his vast number of creations. There are so many questions I would have asked him during our many years of friendship. At least the knowledge I do have of him will not be lost to posterity. With the collaboration of Steve Conti and Bill Seay, as well as the wonderful help from Filomena Bruno, Sascha's relatives and many others, we have presented a fairly complete picture of his artistic talents and abilities. He was not a perfect person; none of us are, but he loved every form of art. Throughout his life there was an insatiable drive to create unusual and beautiful items for the public. Like so many artists, Sascha never seemed to be satisfied. One day, while viewing an Oriental carpet, I commented on the fact that one part of the design seemed to have been left imperfect. Sascha looked at me and said, "Haven't you ever heard that the people of the Middle East always leave their art imperfect, for perfection belongs only to God and, after all, we are mere human beings and can only keep trying." I believe this statement summarizes Sascha's ideals.

Steve Conti: I first met Bill and Dee only a few months prior to Sascha's passing. I had started my Brastoff collection with a very simple, common bowl, purchased at a local antique shop, but knew nothing about the artist. The guys told me the most interesting stories about Sascha and, after gaining their confidence and winning their friendship, I brought up the idea of writing his biography. We all agreed it should be an informative and loving tribute to this remarkable and, unfortunately, misunderstood man. The most precious thing I've gained from this collaboration is a lifelong friendship — born of the hours and hours of conversations and laughter we've shared in producing this book.

~ Chapter 1 ~
From New York to Hollywood

In 1953, the opening night gala for Sascha Brastoff's new West Los Angeles factory and showroom was attended by the "A" list of Hollywood stars. That evening, famed character actor and world renowned art aficionado Edward G. Robinson commented to the press "...Sascha Brastoff is a modern day Cellini; a contemporary DaVinci. There is no medium he cannot conquer." Sascha B had finally "arrived."

Sascha Brastoff actually arrived as Samuel Brostofsky on October 23, 1918, at Saint Ann's Hospital in Cleveland, Ohio. His father, Louis, was a cutter in a clothing factory while his mother, Rebecca (nee Heinovitz), raised Sascha and his three sisters and four brothers.

Ever since Sascha could remember, he had been fascinated by movement, color, texture, and design. When he was seven years old he used an empty coal bin in the cellar as "studio space" to decorate the plain white dinnerware his parents brought over from Europe. Sascha never felt discouraged from exploring his creative side despite daily dishpan scrubbings. His family never seemed to understand his enthusiasm for art and hoped he would show interest in things more productive and useful. We're sure he heard on more than one occasion "you can't make a living by painting plates." Fortunately, Sascha's older sister, Evelyn (Leftofsky), admired his talent and encouraged his creative side. Evelyn would slip S.B. money to purchase art supplies and then hide these early treasures in her bedroom. An inventive Sascha, as a 13-year-old Boy Scout, attained Eagle Scout status by fashioning an elaborate Indian headdress using a "borrowed" horse tail from the neighborhood iceman's reluctant horse (see plates 1 & 2; age 2 and age 13).

Plate 1: Sascha age 2.

Plate 2: Sascha age 13.

Sascha attended Glenville High School in Cleveland and took drama classes under famed producer Ross Hunter (1961's *Back Street* starring Susan Hayward and John Gavin, and *Thoroughly Modern Millie*; 1968). He excelled in his art studies and at 16 was thought to be quite gifted (see plates 3 & 4). His art teachers formed a small private scholarship fund for him to attend the Western Reserve University School of Art in Cleveland. By age 17 his desire to learn the principles and techniques of movement led him to study dance with Edward Caton, who later became ballet master of the Ballet Theatre, and to dance with the Cleveland Ballet for several seasons (see plates 5 & 6).

In 1940, Sascha moved to New York City, set up housekeeping in the artist colony of Greenwich Village and joined the Clay Club located at 4 West Eighth Street (see plate 7). For the next two years he clocked in at Macy's department store every day at 6:00 am, devoting his talents to window dressing. During afternoons he would rush back to his tiny flat and spend the rest of his waking hours sculpting fantastic little whimsical figures out of clay. His window displays were so captivating and popular that Macy's allowed him to incorporate some of his own terra cotta sculptures (see plates 8 –10).

Plate 3: Early drawing by Sascha, age 16.

BAD MANNERS

Plate 4: Early drawing by Sascha, age 14.

Plate 6: Early sketch by Sascha, age 19.
Note signature.

Plate 5: Sascha in the ballet performance of *Afternoon of a Faun* in Cleveland at the age of 18.

Plate 7: Clay Club 1940.

Plate 8: Macy's window display circa 1941, New York City.

Plate 9: "Conversation Piece" by Sascha Brastoff.

Plate 10: "Conversation Piece" #85.

By May of 1941 Sascha had created enough of these "Whimsies" to have a one man showing of the same name at the Clay Club's Sculpture Gallery, running May through June 21st. Numbering 37 in all, these "small, lyrically round and smooth sculptures in natural clay (are) the fruit of Sascha's fancy... voluptuous nymphs, honey bears with angels, impish babies, Medusa, Lady Godiva, etc." Outstanding among the larger works were "Temptation" (Eve flanked by serpent and apple; plate 11), "Neptune's Folly" (an irresistible siren), "Europa and the Bull", expressing Sascha's theory on the child's obvi-

Plate 11: Sascha at work on "Temptation," Clay Club of New York, 1940.

ous parentage (plate 12), and the mythical "Merbaby", part child, part amphibian (see plate 13; collection of Evelyn Leftofsky). *The New York Times* raved "...an extravaganza in miniature — unpretentious but with unmistakable technical evidence of larger scope than finds expression in Brastoff's jesting mood." A comment in the show catalog read "Sascha Brastoff was born in Bangkok, Siam, Petrograd, Russia, or Cleveland, depending on a given mood or occasion."

Sascha's Clay Club show was so successful that every piece sold, some into New York's most prominent and prestigious collections like the Metropolitan Museum, the Whitney Museum, and the personal collection of the Guggenheim family. Several pieces were also purchased for their permanent collection by the Syracuse Museum of Fine Arts. The exhibit garnered Brastoff coverage in *Harper's Bazaar, Art Digest, Time* and other publications. He even received a four page spread in the December 1941 *Life* magazine. On the strength of these accolades, Sascha confidently walked out of Macy's and into the world of fine art (see plates 14 – 19).

Plate 12: "Europa and the Bull".

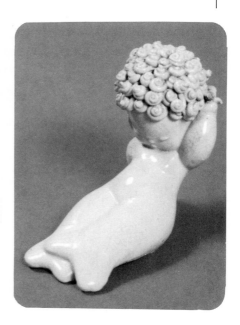

Plate 13: "Merbaby".

Plate 14: "Faun Child".

Plate 15: By Sascha Brastoff, Clay Club Gallery.

Plate 16: "Eternal Question" by Sascha Brastoff.

Plate 17: "Coachman's Holiday" by Sascha Brastoff.

Plate 18: "Serenade" by Sascha Brastoff.

Plate 19: "Joy Ride" by Sascha Brastoff.

In May of 1942, Sascha had to put his career on hold for a loftier mission: Uncle Sam and World War II. Sascha entered the Army's Air Force and reported to Miami, Florida, for basic training. As a sculptor, his extraordinary manual dexterity gave him a high aptitude test rating in mechanics. Never before did science make a more flagrant error. At that time and living in New York City, Sascha didn't even drive a car. Pistons, gears and gaskets were only of interest from a form versus function perspective. Captain George P. Stinchfield, the officer in charge of the "ATC (Air Tactical Command) Contact Caravan" radio variety show, recognized Sascha's unusual talents. Unable to find an army use for his sculpting abilities, Sascha's artistry was put to work in different ways — designing costumes and scenery for many Special Services events to entertain the troops. Like other members of the understaffed department, Sascha had to double as both a designer and a performer. His entree into military show business was performing "an Authentic Voodoo Ritual dance" on March 13, 1943, at the Flamingo Park Bandshell's G.I. Sawdust Revue. According to the program flyer for the event, Sascha was to do "a snake dance with long, slimy, black snakes captured wild in the Everglades. These snakes are positively alive, and positively never have appeared on this stage before." Sascha was a huge hit and was referred to as "the daring young man without a flying trapeze." He later went on to choreograph and perform "The Idol Dance" and the "Cosmic Dance of Shiva" (see plate 20).

Plate 20: Sascha performs "Cosmic Dance of Shiva" for troops.

Sascha was also kept busy drawing war bond posters (see plates 21 & 22), creating elaborate Christmas displays and an extravagant mural (see plates 23 & 24). He received many letters of commendation and a good conduct medal. Sascha was well liked and quickly became known as the camp clown and practical joker. Even during the worst times in the war he could perk up a gloomy group by crowing like a rooster or realistically crying like a baby. On one occasion a Staff Sergeant would not resume his training class until the "infant" was found. S.B. finally 'fessed up, but no harm done. The class loved it! One day Sascha returned from the drill field exhausted. "For thees," he recalled in a phony accent, "I vas brought from Roossia at gr-r-reat expense!" (taken from "To Keep 'Em Flying", 12/12/43).

Plates 21 & 22: Part of a series of posters designed by Sascha for the Air Force.

Plate 23: Sascha working on the mural in the base headquarters.

Plate 24: Wide shot of mural in base headquarters; Miami, Florida.

"G.I. Carmen Miranda"

Sascha's most memorable contribution to wartime entertainment was undoubtedly his creation and portrayal of the "G.I. Carmen Miranda." Intended as a loving spoof of the legendary Carmen Miranda, this novelty number was to be performed in a one week only ATC roadshow, "Contact Caravan's Pan Americana" tribute to South America (June 6–12, 1943.) His act was such an overwhelming hit, Sascha was asked to do "Carmen" wherever he went. Getting into character was no small task even for a seasoned pro like Sascha. The costume, which he designed using an Army blanket to replace the Latin star's tropical prints, and a turban made out of a barracks bag adorned with G.I. mess hall supplies, weighed over 75 pounds! Sascha utilized "over 1000 pieces of equipment... captain's bars, dog tags, bullet shells. His earrings were sergeant's stripes, the fingernails were celluloid tubes painted red, his tights were G.I. woolens dyed red." The entire process of make-up and wardrobe took over two hours. Sascha quipped in a late 1970's interview, "I did two shows a day for so long that from the waist up I was Carmen Miranda and from the waist down Sergeant Brastoff!" (see plates 25 – 26).

Plates 25 & 26: Sascha as "G. I. Carmen Miranda."

The "Contact Caravan" had its first civilian performance on September 16, 1943, at Miami's Lincoln Theater. The event was a war bond benefit and Sascha did Carmen to a standing ovation! Sascha began to receive coverage in *Stars and Stripes* and many local & national newspapers.

Mega-successful New York playwright Moss Hart was asked by Army General Henry H. Arnold to do a play that would "tell Americans what their husbands, brothers and fathers were going through in the Air Forces." Hart spent eight weeks with enlisted men gathering background material. His cast of over 350 was chosen from 7,000 applicants. While in Miami, Hart saw Sascha as "Carmen." He called it "the greatest sight laugh of this century" and wrote a special scene in this new play, *Winged Victory.* Incredibly enough, it would be a little less than six months from the time the idea was conceived until the opening night. When Hart submitted his manuscript to General Arnold for technical approval, no mistakes could be found!

Winged Victory was composed of 17 scenes, tracing the careers of six aviation cadets from their training period to combat duty in the Southwest Pacific. Along with the 300 actual Air Force men, including established actors Edmond O'Brien, Lee J. Cobb, Barry Nelson and George Reeves, were 54 civilian actresses as wives, girlfriends, WACs, etc. Many were actual spouses of the cast! The play opened to a packed house of 1,500 at the Shubert Theater in Boston, November 2, 1943, to rave reviews. *Variety* reported "...*Winged Victory*... is an epoch event in the American theater. It ranks as the finest dramatic production within recent memory, if not for all time..." Another read "...a heart-stopping compound of the blood, sweat and tears expended in winning a war... the biggest thing that playwright Hart has done in a career of notable achievements." The show opened in New York City at the 44th Street Theater on November 20, 1943, to like reviews. *Life* magazine gave it a multi-page feature spread in its November 29, 1943, issue (see plate 27; from the actual magazine).

Plate 27: Sascha as Carmen Miranda in *Life* magazine November 29, 1943.

Sascha's scene takes place on Christmas Eve, the end of a typical training day; our boys throwing an impromptu holiday party. Mess hall "private" Brastoff dons kitchen and militaria to impersonate a singing & dancing Carmen Miranda. All cheer wildly until the festivities are cut short by an enemy raid. Art imitates life once again (see plate 27 from *Life* magazine).

During the *Winged Victory* days he met fellow cast member Howard Shoup. Brastoff and Shoup would become lifelong friends and, upon returning to the states after the war, purchase a modest southern Californian home together (more on their other business alliances later).

In May 1945 *Winged Victory* went out on the road for a six month world-wide tour (see plate 28). Sascha received critical acclaim and lots of newspaper coverage. Seemingly overnight, he was as much an international star as the entertainer he portrayed.

The play's successful Broadway run led to a film version produced in late 1944 by Darryl F. Zanuck at 20th Century Fox in Hollywood and directed by George Cukor (later of 1954's *A Star Is Born* fame). Along with the original cast members, the film starred Gary Merrill and newcomers Judy Holliday and Jeanne Crain. Sascha was called upon once again to do his "G.I. Carmen Miranda" in the film (see plate 29).

Plate 29: Pittsburgh *Press* spread on the movie *Winged Victory*.

Plate 28: Tour schedule for the play *Winged Victory*.

All of the proceeds from both the stage and film versions of *Winged Victory* went directly to the Army Emergency Relief Fund. It raised two million dollars and five million dollars, respectively.

One day while on the set of the movie *Winged Victory*, Fox studio boss Zanuck saw Brastoff doing some sketches between takes. Zanuck found the drawings so intriguing he asked S.B. to come up with some costume designs for Betty Grable's starring role in *Diamond Horseshoe*. Charles Le Maire, executive director of Fox's wardrobe department, endorsed Sascha's talent and used his creations for the eye-filling "Acapulco" and "Pastry Hat" numbers.

Composed of paper, plaster, and chicken wire, the elaborate headgear which crowned the costumes soared four feet high from the top of each showgirl's head. Sascha remarked about one such girl, "She looks like Miss Fire Hazard of 1944!" (see plates 30 – 32). Director George Seaton and Sascha practically came to blows when Seaton ordered the headdresses be cut down. The showgirls just couldn't clear the entrance to their scene. S.B. protested and said, "Raise your sets." Seaton said it would cost the entire production thousands of dollars. "Raise the sets anyway!" Sascha retorted. Seaton was really impressed with this brash, self confident newcomer and said, "this boy has talent...sign him!"

Plate 30: Sascha designed this "Acapulco" costume for film *Diamond Horseshoe*.

Plate 31: Another "Acapulco" original.

Plate 32: Sascha named this showgirl "Miss Fire Hazard of 1944!"

Sascha was signed to a seven year post war contract as a designer and entertainer at 20th Century Fox. Clever Sascha added a special clause allowing him to take time out for sculpting. Even throughout his years of military service, Sascha furloughed back to New York City to sculpt (see plates 33 & 34). On December 18, 1945, Brastoff received an honorable discharge at Mitchell Field in New York. California, here he comes!

Plate 33, Right: "Merchild Fountain" by Sascha Brastoff.

Plate 34, Below: Sascha in New York continues sculpting.

Plate 35: The real Carmen Miranda as "Michele." Costume by Sascha.

Plates 36 & 37: Note chalkboard credit to Sascha for original costume designs.
The film, *If I'm Lucky*, starred crooner Perry Como.

While working at the studio, Sascha designed costumes for the classic 1946 *Razor's Edge* starring Gene Tierney and Tyrone Power (under designer Oleg Cassini) and *If I'm Lucky* starring none other than his idol, Carmen Miranda (see plates 35 – 37).

When Sascha finally met Miss Miranda, who was familiar with his act and admired him, S.B. had just returned from the *Winged Victory* world tour. He quipped, "You can go to Europe now... I've already paved the way!"

Carmen Miranda was reported by Hollywood columnists as saying "Soshint Braystuff, who isss phoney me" and "He is more like Miranda than I am!" Sascha and Carmen became very good friends and remained so until her death in 1955. When they were on the lot at 20th she would often coach him in her mannerisms to improve "the act."

Sascha began to design Carmen's entire personal as well as professional wardrobes (see plates 38 & 39). One such costume was made entirely out of 90 yards of plastic and nylon held together with beads and sequins. It took a dozen girls three weeks to produce the handmade creation. When Miranda was told the material "was only 89 cents a yard" she exclaimed, "Sooo cheap. I buy it right away." (See plate 326 in Price Guide for original sketch.) He also made some of her trademark platform shoes.

Sascha continued to live a bi-coastal lifestyle, going back to New York and the whole Clay Club crowd. In June of 1946 he again entered "Europa and the Bull" in a Sculpture Gallery exhibit and soon began to attract national attention.

An August 1946 newspaper story linked famed bandmaster Bob Crosby (Bing's brother) and Sascha as partners in a Los Angeles dress factory. No other records have been found and we doubt if this venture ever got off the ground.

While Sascha was wrapping up his show biz career, Howard Shoup began a stint at Warner Bros. as a costume designer. His accomplishments would later include five Academy Award nominations.

In late 1947, S.B. negotiated release from his 20th Century Fox contract to follow his passion for producing ceramics. Finally he took the big plunge using his studio salary and opened a tiny ceramics plant in a tin quonset hut located on Sepulveda Boulevard just south of Olympic Boulevard, in West Los Angeles. "Sascha Brastoff Products, Incorporated" was born.

Plate 38: Carmen Miranda gives her approval to Sascha's latest design.

Plate 39: Sascha and Carmen play "Cinderella" with one of her trademark platform shoes.

Chapter 2
Rubbing Elbows

Sascha Brastoff Products, Incorporated proved a force to be reckoned with in the southern California ceramics market. With Hollywood film star Gene Tierney as his first notable client, Sascha soon had them lining up at his factory door. Greer Garson, Ida Lupino, Zachary Scott, Cesar Romero, along with Carmen Miranda, quickly placed orders for custom made artwork. Joan Crawford became a lifetime friend and customer. Mike Romanoff, owner of famed Hollywood eatery "Romanoff's," ordered all of his restaurant's dinnerware. Sascha created a provincial modern set with fish and leaping birds wearing crowns. It was so popular, he received duplicate orders from other celebrities. Sascha believed "dinnerware should have individuality and reflect the interests of the user." He would take samples of chintz, a piece of furniture or anything personal to create one's own pattern. "Buyers from such stores as Marshall Field, Gump's, Neiman-Marcus, and Cannell & Chaffin began to approach me," said Sascha, "and all of a sudden I realized I was in business."

Marion Daniels, a publicist at 20th Century Fox when she met Sascha, was married to *Winged Victory* actor and contract player Mark Daniels. Marion introduced Sascha to his mentor, millionaire industrialist Winthrop B. Rockefeller, in 1947. Rockefeller was the grandson of Standard Oil magnate John D. Rockefeller, Sr. and brother of former New York governor Nelson Rockefeller. At the time, Win had a sort of "decorator's dilemma." He had been searching for some unique ceramic ashtrays to use aboard the family yacht, docked in New York harbor. He asked Sascha to come up with some ideas and was quite pleased with his designs. Win and his wife were patrons of the arts for many famous and even some obscure artists. The Rockefellers commissioned Sascha to paint a mural for their posh Manhattan apartment. He moved in and, working non-stop for three days, produced a magnificent mural that still hangs over one of their several fireplaces! So began the lifelong friendship between Sascha and the Rockefellers (see foreword by Jeannette Rockefeller).

In November 1948, Sascha entered a set of six canapé trays into the Thirteenth National Ceramic Exhibition sponsored by the Syracuse Museum of Fine Arts. The pieces, titled "Abstract Fruit", "Serenade", "Night Ride", "Night Monster", "Fish Monster", and "Sex Monster", won best in show for pottery and a $100 award from the Harker Pottery Company of East Liverpool, Ohio. The six trays (see plate 40) remain today in the National Collection of Contemporary American Ceramics — the permanent collection of the Syracuse Museum (renamed the Everson Museum).

Plate 40: Sascha won Best in Show, 1948, in the 13th National Ceramic Exhibition, Syracuse, NY.

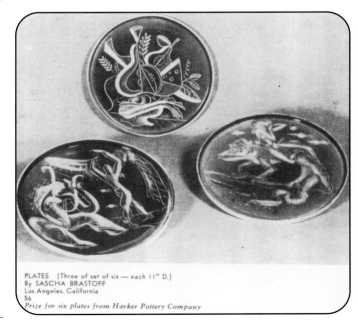

PLATES (Three of set of six — each 11" D.)
By SASCHA BRASTOFF
Los Angeles, California
56
Prize for six plates from Harker Pottery Company

As the business began to grow, it needed more capital for expansion. Win Rockefeller decided to invest in the enterprise and brought to the venture friend E.E. "Ted" Campbell, then vice president of American Ceramics, Incorporated. Campbell became president of Brastoff Products. Rockefeller insisted that a staff of skilled technicians be assembled due to Sascha's lack of experience in mass production. This group included one salesman, three decorators and various administrative personnel (see plates 41 – 46).

Plate 41: Rockefeller assembled this staff of
skilled ceramic technicians and office personnel.

Plate 42: Sascha does quality control with
staff decorator.

Plate 43: Decorator applies
first coat of glaze.

Plate 44: Sascha Brastoff examines details of large charger.

Plate 45: Sascha and a staff decorator discuss new plate design.

Plate 46: Decorator (in foreground) "dips" plate in glaze while another worker arranges shape molds.

The initial line of production consisted of vases, bowls, ashtrays, and ceramic dinnerware (see plates 47 – 62). All were signed with his trademark "Sascha B". Items decorated by Sascha himself were often signed in full and sometimes dated (more on this in Chapter IV; see plates 63 – 74 for early originals). Sascha also created elaborate, hand-formed terra cotta statues (see plates 75 – 86) which sold for over $500 each in the late 1940s & early 50s! Under the reorganized financing, Sascha's factory flourished. More and more orders were received from major department stores across the country; reportedly 1,500 national outlets were selling Sascha! He began a media blitz campaign of newspaper interviews and personal store appearances (see plates 87 – 90). He also did the local television "home living" circuit and began gaining celebrity status (see plates 91 – 96; assorted photos of a newly confident Sascha at work).

Plate 47: An "early" oversized ashtray.

Plate 48: "Early" cachepots.

Plate 49: A selection of "early" ashtrays depicting fruit, vegetable, and leaf designs.

Plate 50: ...more "early" ashtrays.

Plate 51: Ceramic box lids.

Plate 52: "Early" ceramic dinnerware.

Plate 53: Rooster ashtrays, original wholesale price
$4.00 each, in 1949.

Plate 54: "Early" Sascha originals.

Plate 55: Dancing natives were a favorite Sascha
theme in the late 1940's.

Plate 56–58: A group of cachepots decorated with "campy" Western kitsch.

Plate 59: "Life with Father" salt and pepper shakers.

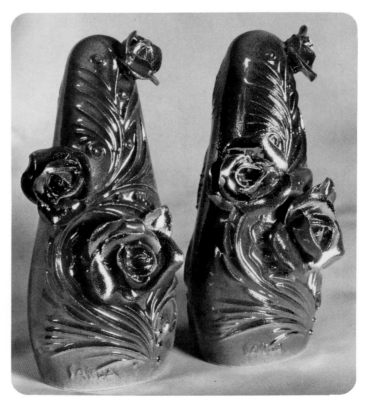

Plate 60: "Early" salt and pepper shakers with applied rosettes.

Plate 61: Sascha was very fond of the Christmas season, as exhibited in his "Littlest Angels" salt and pepper shakers.

Plate 62: Jumbo cup and saucer. Smoke tree pattern, $4.00 wholesale in 1949.

Plate 63: A truly fabulous Sascha original of a plumed horse.

Plate 64: Yet another early, fully signed original.

Plate 65: Made for ballet and film star Vera Zorina.

Plate 66: San Francisco scene made for Gump's department store.

Plate 67: Early Western kitsch.

Plate 68: Another western cowboy design by Sascha himself.

Plate 69: Depiction of doves nesting in floral centerpiece.

Plate 70: An early science fiction theme.

Plate 71: Half man/half plant? ...you decide!

Plate 72: Title unknown, see plate 71.

Plate 73: An "early" original by Brastoff but signed "Sascha B."

Plate 74: "The Flautist"

Plate 75: Front view of hand formed terra cotta figure of 18th century lady. Each curl was hand rolled!

Plate 76: Every pleat and fold of her skirt was meticulously carved by Sascha!

Plate 77: Five more elaborate and unusual ceramic figures by Sascha himself, selling for $3,500.00 and up today. They are extremely hard to find.

Plate 78: Handmade "Native" themed figure.

Plate 79 and 80: Sascha's fascination with the Far East is evident in these two original sculptures.

Plate 81: Sascha's sensational "Belle of the Ball."

Plate 82: Sascha created the fish scale
effect using dental tools!

Plate 83: The "real" Madonna.

Plate 85: This was photographed by Sascha himself in his own back yard.

Plate 84: Another depiction of the Virgin Mary.

Plate 86: A perfect "native" man.

Plate 87: Sascha with a showroom manager in one of the several stores
which showed Sascha's wares across the U.S.

Plate 88: Sascha makes an appearance at Sakowitz in Dallas, Texas.

Plate 89: ...and at Marshall Field in Chicago.

Plate 90: Sascha repeatedly visited Dohrman's in San Francisco, from 1949 through the 1950's. This ad is circa 1955.

Plate 91: Notice pipe cleaner mask behind Sascha.

Plate 92: Sascha's seen here, at home working on an 18" ceramic charger.

Plate 93, Left: Sascha with actor Brian Aherne.

Plate 94, Below: Sascha in the quonset hut.

Plate 95: Sascha copies one of his own original designs.

Plate 96: Sascha and Jerry Schwartz at the first factory.
Note "early" ceramic pieces.

A New Art Studio/Factory for Sascha

Soon the tiny quonset hut became insufficient to keep up with demand. Rockefeller and Campbell negotiated with pottery veteran Tom Hamilton, owner of American Ceramics, Inc. (located at 6300 Compton Avenue, Los Angeles), to set up shop there. Sascha agreed to move his plant and, sadly, a devastating fire on July 10, 1952, snuffed out the fledgling six month old business. Losses were estimated at over $200,000 but fortunately most of the master molds were salvaged. Undaunted, Sascha moved ahead once again. (Tom Hamilton, owner of the L.A. factory, would later open the Winfield Pottery in Santa Monica, California. Sascha did several dinnerware designs anonymously as a thank you.)

At this time, while Rockefeller contemplated his next move to rebuild the business, Sascha farmed out designs to established companies. A fall 1952 issue of *House & Garden* magazine featured a story on Sascha's increasing venture into the lamp field. Designed exclusively for the Crest Company, Chicago, the four pattern collection consisted of rectangular, square or cylindrical shapes in several sizes. "Cheval", a rampant pink horse on a cocoa background; "Ballet Figure", on gray ground; "Foliage", multicolor on green and "Tree of Life", white and gold designs on black. Each of these were previously used on ceramics and dinnerware. All of the lamps ranged in height from 31 to 36 inches and were topped with shades designed by Crest's own Katherine O'Neill. The shades were fashioned from silk shantung, metallics and even novelty fabrics in neutral colors with multicolor trim. Each of the handmade pieces, signed "Sascha B.", retailed from $100 to $200 each in 1952 dollars!

Plate 97, Left to right: Winthrop Rockefeller, Sascha Brastoff, and President Edward E. Campbell study blueprints by architect A. Quincy Jones.

Winthrop Rockefeller recognized Sascha's increasing popularity and seemingly unlimited marketing potential. Never shying away from a sound business venture, the industrialist decided to personally finance a state of the art studio-factory for Sascha. He and Brastoff Company president E.E. Campbell outlined three distinct objectives in the planning and eventual construction of this new plant. E.E. Campbell stated their goals:

1. To erect a factory with offices, sales areas and surroundings which would be in keeping with the unique style and quality of the product produced.

2. To set the standard in the pioneering of California as the true center of ceramic art.

3. To achieve the unusual in comfort, accommodation and general working conditions for a highly skilled staff.

Rockefeller's first choice was a building site near Los Angeles International Airport. Sascha was furious with the suggestion and had a major temper tantrum. Win explained its advantages for shipping to national department stores and receiving supplies not available in southern California. It seems that the ever thrifty Sascha refused to "spend so much money on gasoline just to get to work!" Sascha chose a block of poorly developed land in West Los Angeles not very far from his home. The property was located at the corner of Olympic Boulevard & Colby Avenue and, at the time, S.B. was unaware of the actual street address. Once all of the permit applying, surveying and city planning deals were done the address "11520 West Olympic Boulevard" appeared on the blueprints. An astonished Sascha recalled a time during the European *Winged Victory* tour when he consulted a rather mysterious and theatrical fortuneteller in Italy. She told S.B. he would eventually become very rich and famous. Even Sascha could've predicted that! The psychic scribbled down the numbers "11520" on a scrap of paper, handed it to Sascha and said "one day these will mean something to you." We understand Sascha told that story to many of his guests during the 1953 opening night party of his new factory (see plates 97 – 100).

Plate 98: Scale model of the new state of the art studio-factory.

Plate 99: Scale model of West Los Angeles studio-factory.

Plate 100: New factory
under construction.

Plate 101: The front entrance of the new plant at 11520 West Olympic Blvd.

The architects commissioned for this enormous undertaking were L.A.'s own A. Quincy Jones, A.I.A., and partner Frederick Emmons. The result was a sleek glass and steel structure built in a setting of redwood and desert rock. Occupying 35,000 square feet of floor space, the building boasted of beautifully landscaped gardens with indoor tropical plants and pools and stunning night time lighting effects. It was hard to imagine this was actually a working factory employing dozens of highly skilled artisans. At a cost of over half a million dollars, it was considered the nation's finest studio-factory to date and met all the exacting demands of ceramics production (see plate 101).

The lavish decor of the showrooms magnified the beauty of the commercial art pieces, dinnerware, and "Sascha's Originals." Early press releases declared it "...a challenge to any prospective customer to try to resist purchasing one or several items."

The architects engineered a very functional and versatile suspended iron frame to hold perforated wallboard panels or shelves for displaying the ware. Channel drapery track was fastened to the ceiling studs to cover several floor areas. A set of drapery rollers rode in the overhead channel track and supported any size iron frame desired. These frames were rolled horizontally into any position.

A small table having slots in the bottom was set over the lower rod of the steel frame, preventing frame sway. The table "weight" was additional display space. Wire brackets were used to hang pictures, tiles or plate hangers in the perforated panel. The iron frames and panel boards were painted a dull black to allow for maximum contrast. The small tables were finished in a granite effect using a beige undercoat with a splatter overcoat of white, black and tan. Several styles of wrought iron furniture, tables, and shelving were also used for display. Even four foot lengths of sewer pipe were utilized as pedestals! Large sections of glass paneling on three sides of each showroom maximized use of daylight. All of these techniques are currently used in the leading contemporary department stores and shopping malls. Sascha was really on the cutting edge of design! (See plate 102 & 103; "Prehistoric Fish" in lobby).

A feature attraction at the plant was the Patio Yard where designer experiments and factory seconds were available to customers on a 9 to 5, seven day a week basis. Patrons of the yard found not only seconds but original samples in ceramic and fine china that were produced by Sascha himself but somehow rejected. Because Sascha was so prolific and created designs in such volume many of these "trials" never made it to the final commercial production line. Original, fully signed seconds were offered in the $45 to $50 price range while perfect studio originals sold

Plate 102: Lobby of new factory.

Plate 103: New plant. On wall are oil paintings, ceramic tile panels, plates and ashtrays. Also, sculpture on the tables.

Plate 104: Factory seconds yard or patio yard.

Plate 105: Note display on left.

between $200 and $300 each — back in the early 1950's! Those "seconds" left unsold after a designated time were then destroyed. Sascha would eventually change his production line regularly, giving it a new look (and catalog) every 6 months (see plates 104 –109; all of Patio Yard and gift wrap operation).

Bill Seay fondly tells of a private tour he personally gave to a friend, screen idol Joan Crawford. It seems that Joan wanted to buy a large group of special Christmas gifts and was most interested in the Patio Yard treasures. After spending a delightful couple of hours together, exploring the seemlingly endless selection, Joan made her choices and was ready to pay for them. She turned to Bill and asked if she could purchase them wholesale. He obliged and, as stated, Miss Crawford was a lifelong fan and customer of Brastoff (see letter on page 64).

Plate 106: Lamp patterns seen are "Celadon" ,"Abstract", "Plumed Horse", "Leaf", "Mosaic" "Sun Burst".

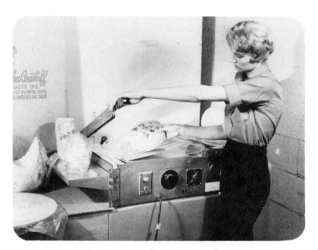

Plate 107: Gift wrap machine.

Plate 108: Gift wrap department.

Plate 109: Ceramic Christmas gifts.

426 NORTH BRISTOL AVENUE
LOS ANGELES 49, CALIFORNIA

January 16, 1954

Bill, dear;

As you know, I've already written you
about that exquisitely, beautiful Sascha Brastoff Ash
Tray... only I have news for you — nobody's going to
use it for that — I won't let them get that near to it...
they're just going to look at it. I also told you how
beautifully it fit in with the black and white color
scheme... and I also told you how good it was to see
you, even briefly on Christmas.

Bless you. I wish I could get in to see
Sascha's things and your paintings... but I'm trying
to do my television show before I leave for Rio and
I'll be gone three months.

However, that does not prevent me from
sending you my very, very best wishes and my delight
at your success on selling the nine paintings.

God bless you. Continued success in 1954
is the wish of a very grateful and devoted,

JOAN CRAWFORD

JC:rb

William Seay
2341 Midvale Ave.
Los Angeles 64, California

Sascha strongly believed that the work environment for his artists should be more pleasant and conducive to creativity than their own homes. His decorators occupied an enormous room flooded with natural light and had their own ample work stations. Above this room was a catwalk or observation platform where visitors would watch by the thousands. The new factory even had a private studio, complete with a bedroom, kitchen, and a bath, for Sascha. Far nicer digs than any small film studio dressing room! (See plates 110 – 119; all of staff decorators and celebrity visitors.)

Sascha created all of the original designs himself and decided which ones would be produced on a commercial basis. His select staff of 40 plus artists would decorate each designated "blank" (bisque fired ceramic), having free reign of their own expression but still following the basic design and color combinations created by Sascha. Each piece was hand painted, often starting with a stenciled design and hand finished. The final product was signed "Sascha B" on his behalf by one of these artisans. All items decorated by the master himself were signed in full "Sascha Brastoff" and sometimes dated. Sascha preferred to design amongst his peers on the main decorating floor. Pieces he produced on the main floor, with his trademark fine gold work, were often signed "Sascha B" like the commercial pieces. Confused yet!? More on the Brastoff marking system in Chapter 4.

Plate 110: Donna Reed at the factory. Artists work on "Jewel Bird."

The new headquarters for Sascha Brastoff Products, Inc., won the 1954 Certificate of Merit for Excellence of Design, awarded by the Southern California chapter of the American Institute of Architects.

All of these elements of vision, design and good business sense came together for a glitzy opening night gala in 1953.

Plate 112: Starlets Joanne Gilbert and Pat Crowley visit the factory and watch artist work on inside design of "Leaf" Bowl.

Plate 111: Joanne Gilbert and Pat Crowley at factory. "Leaf" pattern pitchers.

Plate 113: Raw clay ashtray being removed from mold.

Plate 114: Worker "trims" and "cleans" dry pottery ashtray.

Plate 115: Ashtray gets first background color.

Plate 116: First artist adds second background colors.

Plate 117: Artist hand paints designs.

Plate 118: Sascha looks at a completed ashtray.

Plate 119: Overview of main decorating room.

Lights, Cameras, SASCHA!

The caterers are catering. The florists are arranging. And soon the guests will be arriving — all 620 of them! Specially designed invitations glazed on the underside of a "Sascha B" ashtray were sent in elaborate gift boxes to the "A" list of Hollywood's party set:

You are cordially invited to an

exhibit of fine art in ceramics

by Sascha Brastoff and to the

opening of our studio-factory.

November 18, 1953 5 to 8 p.m.

Among the attendees were Mr. Winthrop Rockefeller, Mr. and Mrs. Edward G. Robinson, Gary Merrill (then married to screen legend Bette Davis), dancer Mitzi Gaynor, actress Marilyn Maxwell, dancer Donald O'Connor, film star Marion Davies (longtime companion of publishing magnate William Randolph Hearst and resident of San Simeon), singer Mario Lanza, funny lady Jane Withers and a reportedly uninvited Zsa Zsa Gabor. The entire original casts of *Winged Victory* (both the stage and film versions) were also invited. When one of Sascha's press agents personally called Marilyn Monroe to invite her to the party, she asked who were the hosts. When the agent replied, "Mr. Brastoff and Mr. Rockefeller" Marilyn remarked "...Rockefeller — isn't he one of those *rich* millionaires?"

Plate 120: November 18, 1953. Rockefeller and Sascha stand under the foyer clock and congratulate each other on the new factory.

Rockefeller delivered this speech to the crowd: "The story of this company began six years ago when a Catholic daughter of an Irish hotelman told me of the extraordinary artistic talents of the son of a Jewish tailor, myself being the Protestant son of a Protestant industrialist. Our factory staff has over 50 multitalented people of all nationalities, races and religions, working together happily and productively."

One overzealous partygoer fell head first into the floor level fish pond. Seay recalls, "she stood up, her Dior gown dripping wet, clutching a plate of soggy Romanoff's hors d'oevres, and climbed out. She walked over to Win Rockefeller and, trying in vain to form a complete sentence, muttered, ...'Winnie, under all that gold you really do have a heart. This is just fabulous...fabulous!'"

Much to his surprise, co-author Bill Seay was put in charge of Sascha's studio during the party. "I wanted to see all of the celebrities — not get stuck there!" While upstairs, a very talkative Harpo Marx wandered into the studio with his wife, former Paramount starlet Susan Fleming, to check out some of the Brastoff originals. Bill was giving the Marxes a private tour of the living quarters and asked if they'd like to see the fabulous hand painted tiles in the bathroom. Seay asked Marx if he'd "like to see Mr. Brastoff's shower." Harpo replied, "why, is *he* in it?!"

The party went well past the 8:00 o'clock estimate, with the "Brastoff Bunch" ending up at the Cocoanut Grove nightclub located in the landmark Ambassador Hotel. Sascha, the Rockefellers, Bill Seay, S.B.'s longtime friend Filomena Bruno, and pal Howard Shoup and others partied to the song stylings of Lena Horne. The entire evening was a big hit and could not have been a better omen to the success of this new venture (see plates 120– 129; all party guests).

Plate 121: Edward G. Robinson, Rockefeller, Mrs. Gladys Robinson, and Sascha.

Plate 122: Edward G. Robinson looks over some of Sascha's
original creations at the opening.

Plate 123: Gary Merrill, Bette Davis's fourth husband, greets Sascha.

Plate 124: Mitzi Gaynor and Sascha.

Plate 125: Marilyn Maxwell and Sascha.

Plate 126: Sascha hams it up with Marion Davies.

Plate 127: Sascha with Jane Withers and husband at opening.

Plate 128: Rockefeller, Zsa Zsa Gabor.

Plate 129: Sascha, Rockefeller and E.E. "Ted" Campbell, president of Brastoff's company.

The magnificent new factory quickly flourished and had visitors from all over the world. Sascha loved his new home and was continually designing, redesigning and modifying new patterns for ceramics and dinnerware. As stated, he preferred to work on the main floor with the other artists. Sascha had always considered himself a social smoker (cigarettes, of course) and, as we know, was very sociable. Bill Seay fondly recalls that "Sascha never bought a pack of cigarettes for himself. Every day, depending on what work station he happened to be at, he would ask someone for a smoke. Soon people would only light up if Sascha wasn't around."

One day, while working incognito with the other staff artists, Sascha felt a little bored and craved some excitement. Perched above on the catwalk was a group of out of towners touring the facility. Sascha remarked on how they "looked like cows grazing in a pasture." S.B., hearing the call of the footlights, decided to pirouette across the entire length of the room while belting out some unidentified operatic notes. After reaching the other side, he grabbed up a plate and, still singing, proceded to twirl back to his work station. The astonished crowd looked on as he continued doing his "Pagli-acci" impersonation. Seay tells, "Sascha leaned over to me and whispered...'that'll give'm something to talk about on the bus back to Peoria!'"

Print, media, and public relations campaigns were heavily increased. Sascha continued to appear at department stores, signing pictures and autographs in the "Sascha B" section. A cover story in the June 6, 1954, Southland Living magazine section of the *Los Angeles Examiner* introduced a new line called "Fantasy in Fabrics." Designed by Sascha based upon earlier ceramic concepts and produced by Seneca Fabrics of New York City, these hand screened cotton fabrics are virtually impossible to find today and are most valuable (see plates 130 & 449 and page 248). On December 23, 1954, Sascha appeared on the local Los Angeles show "City At Night" and brought a most unusual guest — a large and very impressive metal sculpture of a prehistoric fish. This fish was later used along with other metalwork and ceramics in the classic 1956 science fiction hit *Forbidden Planet* starring Walter Pidgeon, Leslie Nielsen, and Anne Francis (see plates 131 – 136).

Plate 130: Fabric.

Plate 131: KTLA's "City at Night" with Kenny Grave, Sascha, and fish from *Forbidden Planet*.

Forbidden Planet co-star Anne Francis, seen here during a May 1955 publicity photo shoot, told author Steve Conti: "I loved Sascha's work and wish I had some of his pieces today!"

Plate 132: "Prehistoric Fish"

Plate 133: "Prehistoric Fish"

Plate 134: "Metal Fossil"

Plate 135: "Sea Ballet"

Plate 136: Sascha creates "Sea Ballet" and refers to original sketch.

After months of preparation, in January of 1955 Sascha unveiled a collection of 21 pieces of original metalwork called "Sculpture in Steel."

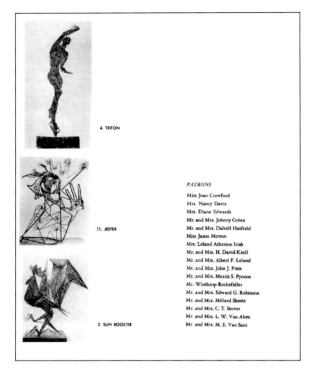

PATRONS

Miss Joan Crawford
Mrs. Nancy Davis
Mrs. Diane Edwards
Mr. and Mrs. Johnny Green
Mr. and Mrs. Dalzell Hatfield
Miss Jason Herron
Mrs. Leland Atherton Irish
Mr. and Mrs. H. David Kroll
Mr. and Mrs. Albert F. Leland
Mr. and Mrs. John J. Preis
Mr. and Mrs. Morris S. Pynoos
Mr. Winthrop Rockefeller
Mr. and Mrs. Edward G. Robinson
Mr. and Mrs. Millard Sheets
Mr. and Mrs. C. T. Stover
Mr. and Mrs. L. W. Van Aken
Mr. and Mrs. M. E. Van Sant

SCULPTURE IN STEEL

1. Sea Ballet
2. Sun Rooster
3. Prehistoric Fish
4. Triton (figure)
5. Illusion
6. Totem
7. Owl God
8. Joust
9. Landscape
10. Flaming Bush
11. Jester
12. Metal Fossil
13. Copper Torso
14. Reclining Figure
15. Harvest
16. Ariel
17. Idol
18. Demon
19. Jungle Snare
20. Coq D'or
21. Spring Growth

Special Exhibit

Butterfly Fish
*Recently on display at the Cranbrook Academy
of Fine Arts, Scripps College and the Sculpture
Center in New York*

Already recognized as one of the nation's finest ceramists, Sascha Brastoff has long been interested in the field of steel sculpture, and recently returned from New York's Sculpture Center where he devoted many months to creating the twenty-one new pieces shown in this exhibit.

A few years ago, artists working in this medium modelled first in wax or clay and then had their handiwork cast in a foundry. Today, the advanced process of acetylene welding permits a more direct approach. It results in natural colorings from the materials used, such as yellow and pink from bronze and red from copper, where before only black was possible.

Mr. Brastoff has been among the first to utilize such decorative notes within the main element. His *Prehistoric Fish*, for example, presents individual hammered copper scales, each encrusted with swirls of pink bronze woven together in a network, contrasted with head and tail of black steel.

Particularly unique is the artist's *Triton* which features many-textured steel prongs and points; the barbed steel, built from drops of hot metal, offers the surrealistic illusion of soft flesh.

These impressionistic experiments in metal sculpture form the latest art interpretations by a superb young craftsman who has excelled previously as a painter, costume designer, goldsmith, dancer, mime and decorator. Brastoff's fascinating excursions into the ceramics field served as a potent force in the revival of ceramic art and won his efforts a place in some of the nation's leading museums and private collections. This newest pilgrimage to metal art is another striking indication of his irresistible urge to explore new mediums and forms of expression.

Plate 137: Original brochure from January 1955.

Sascha had long been interested in steel sculpture. Up until just a few years prior, artists first had to model their pieces in wax or clay and then have it cast in a foundry. Brastoff was among the pioneers to experiment with an acetylene welding torch (as early as 1940). The result was in natural colorings from the materials used: pink and yellow from bronze and red from copper. Before this technique, only charred black was achieved. Noteworthy in the group were "Triton", (also used in *Forbidden Planet),* "Joust" (see plate 138), "Coq D'or" (see plate 140), "Jester" (see plate 139), and "Sun Rooster" (see plate 141). "Illusion," along with "Prehistoric Fish," was also featured in *Forbidden Planet* (see plate 142). The "Sun Rooster" was donated to the Los Angeles County Museum of Art by Rockefeller in the name of Mrs. Leiland Atherton Irish in the spring of 1955. Mrs. Irish was a socially prominent patroness of the arts and very much a fan of Sascha's work.

Sascha was now being inundated with

Plate 138: "Joust".

Plate 139: "Jester".

Plate 140: "Coq D'or."

Plate 141: Presentation of "Sun Rooster" steel sculpture to Los Angeles County Museum. Left to right: Mrs. Morris S. Pynoos, Sascha, Mr. Marvin Roso, Curator Los Angeles Museum, Mrs. Leiland A. Irish, Mr. Jean de la Cour, Director Los Angeles Museum.

Plate 142: "Illusion" used in the motion picture *Forbidden Planet*.

requests for large, specially commissioned artwork. Later on in his career this would become his mainstay. Adhering to this hectic schedule of personal appearances and the demand for new designs seemed at times overwhelming. In the mid 1950's, a prized gift to the new state of Israel was a large ceramic charger depicting the 12 tribes of Israel. This was presented during a 35 day goodwill tour to the country's president, Itzhak Ben-Zvi, on behalf of the Los Angeles Jewish community. Two other notable items were specially produced for mentor Win Rockefeller. One was for the Tower Building that he owned in Little Rock, Arkansas. Titled "The Quest", the completed bronze and stainless steel sculpture stood 14 feet high! Sascha is pictured here with workers loading it up for shipment (see plates 143 & 144). The 24 inch prototype is currently owned by co-author DeWayne Bethany and is pictured in plate 279. Another massive art piece was a mural for the Rockefeller's Morrilton, Arkansas, ranch *Winrock*. It flanks one side of the Rockefeller's lakeside boathouse (see plate 291 for prototype). Another popular request was for the 14K gold and precious stone jewelry created exclusively for close friends like Mrs. Rockefeller, Joan Crawford, and Gypsy Rose Lee (consult Chapter 3; plates 216–221).

In the late 1950's, Sascha was asked to pro-

Plate 143: "The Quest" sculpture being prepared for shipment to Little Rock, Arkansas. The model for this sculpture was retained by Sascha and later purchased by author DeWayne Bethany.

Plate 144: "The Quest" sculpture being prepared for shipment to Little Rock, Arkansas.

duce a series of swimming pool tiles for Toni Mannix, whose husband, Eddie, was second in command at Metro-Goldwyn-Mayer under the notorious Louis B. Mayer. Sascha completed a set of 20 different fish designs and installed them along the sides of her pool. The finished pieces were fabulous... until the pool was filled with water and light refraction caused the images to vanish. Sascha was quite surprised but Toni was furious, claiming S.B. knew this would happen all along and did it as a gag!

Henny Backus, wife of character actor and "Mr. Magoo" voice Jim Backus, was a regular at the Brastoff plant. She had the same gift giving dilemma as all Hollywood types — find the perfect gift without fear of duplication. One Christmas, Henny bought several tall unglazed ceramic cats from Sascha's factory and, with the help of Bill Seay's father, custom decorated each piece, signing 'Henny' on the bases (where 'Sascha B' would be.) Sascha loved Henny and gave her his approval and blessings. It's so hard to be original and so easy to be outdone in Tinseltown!

Character actress Hazel Shermet (wife of "Mr. Ed" and "All in the Family" writer Larry Rhine) told Steve Conti how Sascha "saved her life one day." Hazel found a fabulous lamp at the exclusive Melrose Place design shop owned by decorator Paul Ferrante. Hazel wasn't sure if the vintage lamp, which cost several hundred dollars, would harmonize with the furnishings in her home. She asked a Ferrante assistant if she could have the lamp for a weekend to see how it looked. He obliged and, with great care, Hazel took the lamp home. When the piece was accidentally broken by a servant, a frantic Hazel called Sascha for his help. S.B. restored the lamp to its pristine condition and, when Hazel returned it to the design shop, it appeared as if nothing had happened. Needless to say, Miss Shermet was thrilled with the outcome, not to mention that the service was performed at no charge!

Sascha became very proficient in his gold application and could paint it on "as thin as a strand of gold wire." He felt that gold could improve the look of any piece. Seay recalls when Sascha and several of his decorators were examining a group of charred and seemingly unsalvageable ceramics hot from the kiln. The section manager suggested the hopeless pottery be destroyed but Sascha protested. "More gold!" he shouted. "All they need is more gold! My public LOVES anything with lots of gold!"

Sascha had a uniquely sharp and satirical wit. Few could keep up with his many one-liners. Brastoff company president Ted Campbell had two energetic and rather annoying young sons. One day, while decorating a large tile, S.B. was tired of the two hovering about, asking inane questions and being, in general, a nuisance. Finally he turned to the boys and said, "why don't you go and do something constructive — like setting your father on fire!" Seay remarks, "working with Sascha and his 'acid' sense of humor was like hanging around with Monty Wooley in *The Man Who Came to Dinner*."

In August of 1956, Bill Seay was promoted to manager of the lamp manufacturing division. Once again Sascha produced lamps with the same designs as his successful ceramic series, to complement and enhance any room decor (see catalog reprints; platepages 306 & 307).

Among the celebrities and famous artists to visit the West L.A. factory in 1957 was France's Marcel Vertés. Mr. Vertés arrived unannounced one day and was completely unrecognized by Sascha's young receptionist. He was nearly turned away until Bill Seay (in Sascha's absence due to a sales trip) greeted the esteemed visitor and gave him the run of the plant. Vertés spent several days painting plates and doing his own experimenting. Two of these items (a plaque owned by Seay and a plate owned by Bethany) are pictured along with rare photos shot by Bill Seay (see plates 145 & 423).

One of Winthrop Rockefeller's personal goals, as early as the quonset factory, was to develop, produce, and successfully market a line of fine American porcelain dinnerware. The long established competitors were, of course, England, France and Germany. Most American manufacturers, like Bauer, Homer Laughlin and Vernon Kilns, sold ceramic place settings. Sascha designed simply elegant pieces that were expensive in the mid 1950s when offered at up to $32.50 per 5-piece place setting (see plate 146). Sascha had always made ceramic dinnerware, like the popular and ever-so-common "Surf Ballet", dipped in real gold and platinum (see page 236 & 237). His porcelain dishes could rival anything the British and the Europeans were producing. In our shopping experience, these pieces are difficult to find today (see plates 147 – 156).

Plate 145: World famous artist Marcel Vertés worked at Sascha's studio for several days as a compliment to Sascha. Mr. Vertés produced a tile panel now owned by author Bill Seay and a raised design — white on white sun face plate — now owned by author DeWayne Bethany.

Plate 146: Sascha's Fine China.

Plate 147: An assortment of Sascha's fine china.

Plate 148: "Winrock" fine china.

Plate 149: "Allegro."

Plate 150: "Leaf" design ceramic dinnerware.

Plate 151: More ceramic "Leaf" settings.

Plate 152: "Rondo" ceramic dinnerware.

Plate 153: Chemical lab and test equipment for porcelain dinnerware.

Plate 154: "Smoke Tree" porcelain dinnerware.

Plate 155: "Fans" fine china.

Plate 156: "Jade Tree" china.

Accolades continued to pour in from all over the world. One 1957 Pittsburgh newspaper article referred to Sascha as "a sort of minor Leonardo da Vinci." The December 1958 southern California sportsman's magazine *Club* called him a "man for all seasons." Brastoff kept up the public appearances, now heavily promoting his new dinnerware. In a 1958 Seattle article, Dorothy Neighbors commented "…eight years ago when Brastoff first came to Seattle (for a department store visit) he was just beginning to be known. Now he displays all the poise and brains of a tycoon as well as an artist. The shy, smiling person has disappeared… in his place the person of importance." (See plate 157, a 1958 TV appearance; plates 158 – 163, store shots.)

Plate 157: Sascha does a second KTLA TV show. The doll figure is now owned by author Steve Conti.

Sascha was a huge international success and Sascha B a household word. His factory now employed over 100 of the top china and pottery workers in the United States. Sascha commented: "So what if I have a lot of celebrity clients and friends?" It just wasn't enough anymore. Or perhaps it was too much? Sascha would feel unmotivated and bored one day and exhilarated the next. Not new for a temperamental artist. So little remained to explore and conquer. Almost suddenly greed replaced satisfaction; financial gain overshadowed creative happiness.

Winthrop Rockefeller had always been most generous with Sascha and never denied any of his requests. When Sascha wanted a new pug mill for clay mixing (in the mid-1950s, a $20,000 expense), Rockefeller without protest wrote a check. Win allowed Sascha to do what he believed he was put on this planet for — simply, to create.

Sometime in 1961 Sascha was encouraged to renegotiate his "deal" with Rockefeller. This dissatisfaction was instigated by the selfish influence of one of Sascha's friends. S.B. acknowledged Rockefeller's generosity over their 15 year alliance. Sascha was always handsomely paid and never had

Plate 158: Sascha sketching at a department store, circa 1957.

to worry about the daily operation of the business. One day, after driving to Palm Springs to visit the Rockefellers, Sascha's motor blew up in the desert heat. Win and Jeannette sent a limousine to retrieve him and the next day bought him a new convertible to drive back to Los Angeles. Now that's generous!

Sascha deluded himself into thinking this could last forever. He had no idea the enormous overhead of a 35,000 square foot "city unto itself" meant the factory always operated at a loss. Sascha's friend insisted that he demand a cut of the company profits in lieu of his guaranteed salary. Win reluctantly agreed and a meeting was scheduled for sometime after the next fiscal quarter. Instead of giving Sascha a profit check, Rockefeller presented him with a bill for more than $10,000 in company losses! Sascha left his beloved company in a state of shock. His friend, within a short time, would leave him, too.

Press releases in 1962 revealed a nervous breakdown and disappearance into the High Sierras. Sascha proclaimed "money is not enough." This Phoenix would once again be reborn!

Plate 159: A "Sascha" display, circa 1958.

Plate 160: Don't fight, ladies, there's plenty for all of you!

Plate 161: Sascha entertains shoppers with an impromptu drawing.

Plate 162: Sascha arranging a department store display.

Plate 163: Display at Wanamaker's, Philadelphia.

🌿 Chapter 3 🌿
Out There On My Own

For the first time in Sascha's life he felt desperately alone. Fortunately, he had the love and support of friends Howard Shoup and Filomena Bruno. Along with his deep depression and overwhelming sense of loss, Sascha battled what is currently known as agoraphobia. He confined himself to his modest West Los Angeles home and occupied his time by doodling sketches and creating a fabulous cactus & succulent garden. There were conflicting rumors around town that Sascha had died or perhaps gone insane. Through much perseverance, Filomena and Howard finally convinced Sascha to seek psychiatric treatment and got him into therapy. He gradually got stronger with each ensuing month of treatment. His confidence in his talent was slowly restored. Sascha concentrated primarily on charcoal and pastel drawings, producing some of his greatest work to date. By 1965 he was creating fantastic mythical images, costume designs, religious icons and portraits on construction paper, cardboard and even newspaper backgrounds. Sascha's real therapy was through the free expression in these hundreds and hundreds of drawings — many of which he destroyed as though attempting to kill the very demons they represented. He tried painting in oil — a medium he was not entirely comfortable with. While helping to close out Sascha's estate, we found a stack of unsigned oils in a backyard storage shed of very "dark" and mysterious abstract images. The pastels and oil paintings pictured in this book were those he favored and subsequently spared. We consider them most rare and valuable (consult Price Guide; pages 166-181).

WINROCK FARMS
ROUTE 3
MORRILTON, ARKANSAS

July 9, 1962

Mr. Sascha Brastoff

Dear Sascha:

    All that glitters is not gold!

    Our Fifth Annual Production Sale, though possibly less spectacular than last year's, was a more balanced one; and we were delighted to see so many new bidders and buyers. Over and above this we, if possible, had more fun than ever.

    We hope that you share our feeling about the Sale and will, therefore, enjoy having the enclosed souvenir folder.

    Already we are looking forward to next year, and hope that you will mark your calendar now for the second Saturday in May and our Sixth Annual Sale.

    With all good wishes,

    Sincerely,

    Winthrop Rockefeller

Enc.

Although they dissolved their working partnership, Rockefeller and Brastoff remained close friends. Win cared a lot about Sascha and was very concerned about his well being, as evidenced by their letters (see pages 89 – 91).

WINROCK FARMS
ROUTE 3
MORRILTON, ARKANSAS

August 7, 1963

Mr. Sascha Brastoff

Dear Sascha:

Following our custom, Jeannette and I have had souvenir folders made up of our Sixth Annual Sale at Winrock.

We hope that yours will serve the dual purpose of a memento of the occasion, and a reminder for you to mark on your calendar now the second Saturday in May, 1964, the date of our Seventh Annual Santa Gertrudis Sale.

We are glad you could be with us, and with all good wishes,

Sincerely,

Winthrop Rockefeller

Enc.

WINROCK FARMS
ROUTE 3
MORRILTON, ARKANSAS

January 28, 1964

Mr. Sascha Brastoff

Dear Sascha:

My ten happy years in Arkansas suggested to us that a celebration taking note of the anniversary would afford us an opportunity to have a party and at the same time express to our friends, associates, and employees, our appreciation for the important part that they had played in making these the most happy years that they have been.

Little did I expect that this occasion would be one that would be marked by anything other than our own plans, so you can well imagine how overwhelmed I was when a group of my friends from around the State decided to honor me with a dinner in Little Rock. I can assure you I was thrilled by this warm expression of confidence and friendship and quite frankly, just between us, it did my ego no end of good!

The several celebrations drew most pleasant press coverage and were the inspiration for certain publications that have been most charmingly done. All of these things we have gathered together and put in a souvenir folder. It has occurred to me that a few of my close friends -- whether they were a party to or not -- might enjoy having this folder. So, at the risk of seeming to be tooting my own horn, I am taking the liberty of sending it to you and hope that you will enjoy it.

With all good wishes,

Sincerely,

Winthrop Rockefeller

Enc.

91

It was during his recovery that Sascha decided to try metal sculpture again. S.B. was one of the first artists to create directly in metals using an acetylene torch. One day, while rummaging around a junk yard in Gardena, California, he discovered a magical beauty in titanium and magnesium, the standard for space age metals. Only Sascha could find inspiration in the discarded remains of a local foundry! Sascha began to experiment with these metals along with copper, brass, zinc, and aluminum. He took his life in his hands when he started working with highly flammable magnesium — a key ingredient in the manufacture of explosives. Magnesium's high strength-to-weight and stiffness-to-weight ratios were as appealing to Brastoff as they were to modern automotive, aircraft, and aerospace engineers. The metal had a desirable bright silvery color. Sascha was enthused and the "experts" were skeptical. Metallurgists and foundrymen questioned its workability. Sascha's neighbors questioned his sanity as the constant backyard explosions almost drove them crazy. After much persistence, hard work, and dedication, Sascha proved he could control the gleaming metal. The result was in a kind of "sculpture that speaks to all" (*Los Angeles Herald Examiner*, week of January 31, 1965). Collectively known by Brastoff as "Perceptive Sculpture," the artworks are actually made of several metals formed in a molten stage in a high temperature furnace. The process results in almost any abstract shape and metallic hue. Some are a rose gold, some a dull copper and others silvery. Each piece was one of a kind and signed by Sascha. The collection was made available commercially through exclusive showrooms (see plate 164). Ranging in size from 6 inches to 3 feet, they were priced from $25.00 to $150.00 each. Production was somewhat limited as Sascha could only make approximately four smaller ones or one larger sculpture per day. Sascha proclaimed, "my sculptures could do double duty as a modern day Rorschach test. This is my answer to the tomato can school of Pop Art that seems so acceptable today."

Plate 164: Ad slick for Sascha's "Perceptive Sculpture" circa 1965.

The official unveiling in Los Angeles of these experimental sculptures was given by art expert Harold Cunningham. Hal was the art director for the exclusive Ivory Tower Restaurant and Art Gallery in Santa Monica, California. The event, held on Sunday, April 25, 1965, included "Phoenix" (mounted on a telephone pole base and priced at a hefty $5,000.00), "Jungle Night" and "Moongate". All of the pieces were well received and part of the collection sold. Mr. Cunningham personally created all of the unique art displays and exotic flower arrangements.

Meanwhile, down at the Brastoff factory, it seemed like business as usual, with staffer Jerry Schwartz running the operation and Eddie Kourishima as artistic director (later opening the Venice Clay Shops; see Price Guide, page 245 and plate 444). Ted Campbell remained as president until his sudden and untimely death. Upon Sascha's exit, the company secured the right to use the "Sascha B" name as a registered trademark and the rooster (chanticleer) logo (refer to Chapter 4 for details). Over the next 10 years they would simply reissue popular old designs of Sascha's or, in an attempt to increase income, purchase items from trade shows and simply affix a paper label or etch Sascha's name onto them (see page 203 & 294 and plate 369 for explanation of Resin or Resolite pieces). In an effort to reduce production costs and overhead, Jerry Schwartz moved the operation to 12530 Yukon Avenue, Hawthorne, California, around 1964, where it remained until closing in 1973.

Sascha's outlook on life improved dramatically with the instant acceptance of his new art form. He hired a publicist to tell the world he was back, never confessing his nervous breakdown. Sascha simply admitted being "burned out" and "used up." He said, "I put on my wings and, like Icarus, got too close to the Sun. I needed a plunge in the ocean of new beginnings to cool off." His home life changed dramatically, too, with the addition of a new "roommate." (See plate 165.) Liz was Sascha's pet monkey and one can easily guess who was her namesake! Sascha had a precarious relationship with some of his neighbors, due partly to the magnesium explosions and partly to the antics of his monkey. On one occasion, Sascha and a neighbor argued over the primate feasting on the man's fruit trees. The discussion continued into the gentleman's living room where Sascha found an entire wall of his ceramics. S.B. had no idea the man liked his work, much less collected it. "I've been buying them for years from your seconds yard," the neighbor said. When Sascha ordered they be taken down, the perplexed man complied. Sascha then took a marking pen and proceeded to sign and date each one declaring, with his fabulous sarcastic wit, "NOW they're worth something!"

Plate 165: Sascha with Liz in 1966.

Sascha honed down his talent to control and sculpt this unpredictable new find, magnesium. A select group of these masterpieces was unveiled at a black tie premiere on October 1, 1966. Held at the Dalzell Hatfield Galleries located in the Ambassador Hotel, downtown Los Angeles, the event titled "Moon Age Sculpture" was hosted by Mrs. Winthrop Rockefeller. Jeannette left her husband on the campaign trail back in Arkansas where he was running for governor. The guest list included Joan Crawford, Jim and Henny Backus, Suzanne Pleshette (a longtime client of designer Howard Shoup), The Sinatras (Frank and new bride Mia Farrow), Rita Hayworth, Liberace, Mrs. Zeppo Marx, and the entire production staffs of television's "Star Trek," "Lost In Space," and "Time Tunnel."

The gallery's program quoted Sascha "Magnesium is an element of the sea and it emerges in sculptured form with the same surging liquid strength and, like the sea, embraces many elements. Sculpture can sing of man and the machine in quest of space."

Among the exhibited pieces were "Visitation" (owned by DeWayne Bethany), "Circle Of Fate", "Fleur De Lune", "Survival", "Moon Sprite" and "Faith-Eternal" (see plates 166 – 171). Each piece was distinct and mounted on natural bases of bark, driftwood, sun bleached animal skulls, and coral. Finishes were in a variety of tones — tarnished rose gold, copper, brass, oxidized platinum, and more. A hand-etched brass signature plate was affixed to each sculpture (see plates 172–174; welding shots).

Plate 166: "Visitation".

Plate 167: "Circle of Fate".

Plate 168: "Fleur de Lune".

Also on exhibit was a select group of fine 14K gold and precious stone jewelry — each one of a kind and handmade using the lost wax process. Sascha designed and created his jeweled wonders exclusively for close friends, especially Jeannette Rockefeller, the premiere's hostess. In a later interview, Sascha admitted to carving many of these stones himself.

A reporter covering the event referred to it as "The Brastoff Blastoff." The show was such a success it was held over "due to unusual interest" with sales into March 1967.

A private showing was arranged prior to the black tie premiere for His Eminence, James Francis Cardinal McIntyre of the Los Angeles Archdiocese. Cardinal McIntyre was shown a five foot crucifix called "Crucifix From Outer Space — Whither Goest Thou?" The meeting was held at a luncheon in Mrs. Rockefeller's suite at the Beverly Hills Hotel. The Cardinal described this first magnesium crucifix as "breathtaking." The piece was never offered for sale and we don't know where it is today.

Sascha was once again on top of the world. Press releases proclaimed him "the Phoenix up from the ashtrays."

At this same time, Sascha received a heartfelt thank you from Universal Pictures for loaning the artwork prominently displayed in the 1967 thriller *Games*. The film starred Simone Signoret, newcomers James Caan and Katharine Ross (just before the smash hit "The Graduate") and garnered wide critical acclaim.

Plate 169: "Survival".

Plate 170: "Faith-Eternal".
Collection of Daniel E. Fast, M.D., Los Angeles.

Plate 171: "Moon Sprite".

95

Plate 172: Sascha in full welding regalia.

Plate 173: Sascha welds a "mammoth" sculpture.

Plate 174: Sascha deep in creation.

St. Augustine-by-the-Sea's Thirteen Foot Cross — A Monumental Achievement

The accolades Sascha received from the Dalzell Hatfield show garnered him the greatest commissioned work of his career. On March 9, 1966, St. Augustine-by-the-Sea Episcopal Church, located in Santa Monica, California, was destroyed by an arsonist. The original little redwood church was founded in 1887 when Santa Monica was populated by less than 2,000 people. The church was built by itinerant carpenters using very simple and traditional cruciform lines.

The Reverend Robert E. Hoggard, Rector and architect John Stewart Detlie chose Sascha to design and construct all ecclesiastical art for the new sanctuary. Rev. Hoggard had attended the "Moon Age" show in October 1966 and felt Brastoff was the right man for this earthly job. Sascha designed a 13 foot tall and 7 foot wide textured, welded steel cross titled "I Am the Light." The three dimensional, many faceted, open ended cross was built in 6 interlocking sections for gold plating. The plating process was done in a specially designed 8 foot tank. The cross was then assembled and installed in the sanctuary where it appears to be suspended "between heaven and earth." It was positioned in the center of the sanctuary with pews on all four sides. When Sascha constructed the 4 foot model for this cross he let the molten steel trickle down, referring to it as "tears of sorrow" or the "blood of the steel." Sascha also created four candlesticks that were placed in "tension" with the great floating cross — two on the altar and two on the floor. The gold plated Eucharistic candleholders on the altar were 44" tall and were intended to "bring light to the holy meal, or communion." One has a figure walking on the earth; the other has a figure with arms uplifted, ascending among the clouds. The two gold plated pavement, or floor, lights were to be taller than any person who would stand in the sanctuary. They were 6 feet tall (excluding their 2 foot candles) and detailed "the Lord's creations: the sun, moon, stars, lightning, birds, fish, ani-

Plate 175: The altar at St. Augustine-by-the-Sea, circa 1967.

Plate 176: The great cross of gold.

mals, and people suspended in an organic metal rhythm" (see plates 175–179).

Sascha created fabulous insets to adorn the two church pulpits (see plates 180–184). The gold plated altar railings were also Sascha's (see plates 185–186.) He did all of the welding himself using a new, triple-torch method combining heli-arc, arc-welding (electric) and oxy-acetylene torches. After shaping and welding, the objects were first copper and nickel plated, then a layer of gold plate was set on.

The creations were first publicly shown on July 19, 1967, at Lincoln Certified Welders, 4130 Glencoe Avenue in Venice, California. The cocktail party reception was attended by actor/director John Cassavettes, the Backuses, costumer Edith Head, Mrs. Nat King Cole, gallery owner Ruth Hatfield, Howard Shoup, and many others. The guest list included some 300 names!

The official dedication of these church decorations was held on Saturday, October 28, 1967, with the Right Reverend Francis Eric Bloy, Episcopal Bishop of the Diocese of Los Angeles, officiating. In a thank you letter written by Rev. Hoggard, he told Sascha "...more than 2,000 people attended the dedication services and many more thousands will also see and enjoy them [the great cross and altar adornments]. They stand as a witness to the skill and dedication of people such as yourself." At a cost of $250,000 (out of the $2 million restoration budget), this was the most expensive installation of Sascha's work we know of! The design of the cross was so popular Sascha made 4" replicas to be worn by the notable personalities who requested them.

At the same time as the cross dedication, Sascha had his first one-man showing of the sketches and drawings he produced during his recovery. Held at the Aaron Brothers La Cienega Galleries in West Hollywood, California, the pastel, ink, watercolor, and lacquer pictures remained on display October 4 – 29, 1967. They ranged in price from $90.00 to $150.00 each. Some of these are featured in this book and are in our personal collections.

Plate 177: Altar candle holder is 44" tall at St. Augustine-by-the-Sea.

Plate 178: Detail of altar candle holder at St. Augustine-by-the-Sea.

Plate 179: Altar candle holder is 44" tall at St. Augustine-by-the-Sea.

Plates 180–186: Gold plated podium insets and altar rails.

Sascha's next grand scale commissioned work was for the Angelo Pappas family in honor of Mr. and Mrs. Louis H. Pappas. The sculpture, titled "Supplication", was to adorn the all-faiths chapel in the Centinela Valley Community Hospital in Inglewood, California. S.B.'s overall concept expressed a unity of all religions reaching toward one God. It was declared "...no man is a stranger in this room of meditation." The sculpture, dedicated in December 1969 to celebrate Christmas, is still there today (see plate 187).

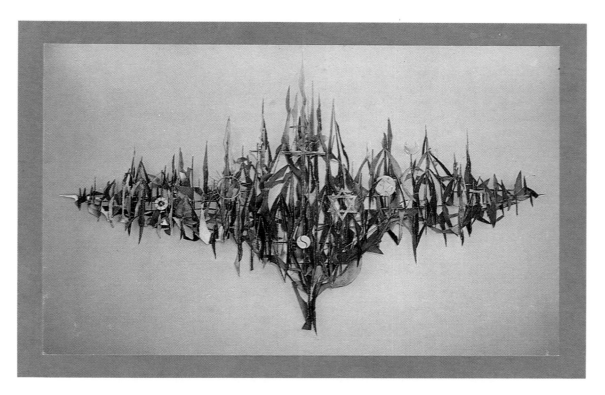

Plate 187: "Supplication."

SUPPLICATION
Chapel, Centinela Valley Community Hospital

The Sculpture Expressing Symbols of the World Religions United in a Common Bond that reaches to One God —
Sascha Brastoff, Sculptor

BUDDHISM

INDIAN

CHRISTIANITY

TAOISM

JUDAISM

HINDUISM

ISLAMISM

SHINTOISM

ESPLANADE — A New Concept in Retailing

Take four great minds with successful track records, put them in a setting of old world charm with contemporary touches and you have Esplanade. The literal translation in Spanish is "total artistic environment." And that's what Sascha, longtime friend Howard Shoup, businessman George Fencl, and financier Robert Young (not of "Marcus Welby" fame) created in 1969.

Sascha found a fabulous 1920's Spanish style building by architect John Byers and turned the property into an open air shopping extravaganza. Located at 246 26th Street in the posh Brentwood area of Los Angeles, Sascha converted one of the rooms for his creations. He lined the walls in black velvet, did the floor in white marble, and used hidden spotlights to illuminate several lucite display cases. Offered for sale were one of a kind original metal sculptures, miniature gold plated sculptures, paintings, and jewelry.

Sascha asked Bill Seay if he would be the consulting interior designer for this project. Of course Bill consented, garnering the finished product a feature spread in the Fall 1969 issue of *Architectural Digest* magazine (see plates 188–191).

Plate 188: Esplanade patio.

Plate 190: Esplanade jewelry showroom.

Plate 189: Esplanade inner patio.

Plate 191: Esplanade showroom. Model for "Supplication," in Centinela Valley Community Hospital Chapel, on far wall. The cross in the window is now in the Arthur Green collection. The bronze "Percheron" horse on the table is now in the collection of author DeWayne Bethany. The large fish sculpture was used in the classic science fiction picture *Forbidden Planet*.

Howard Shoup's fashion salon, once the living room of the original house, included antique French furniture (procured and offered for sale by Bill Seay), a fireplace, and shuttered windows as focal points for the display of his clothing and accessories. Shoup had designed wardrobes for the likes of Judy Garland, Jane Powell, June Allyson, Natalie Wood, Elizabeth Taylor, and Debbie Reynolds. Filomena Bruno produced many of Howard's creations during their long friendship. Howard was nominated five times for the Academy Award and was the first president, re-elected four other times, of the Costume Designer's Guild — talk about a track record! His clientele remained not only loyal but very enthusiastic about his latest venture.

The art gallery, formerly a shed, was beamed and whitewashed and outfitted with sliding glass doors that opened onto the gazebo. The patio area also had glass display cubicles for current fashions and Sascha's new "Horti-sculpture" pieces — hand carved Styrofoam artware filled with exotic plant life. In fact, Sascha designed the massive wrought iron gates and display "cages."

Jeannette Rockefeller, a governor's wife since Win had been elected governor of Arkansas, arranged a fabulous opening party for the gallery. In a large green and white striped tent adjoining the gallery, played the Henry Shead Jazz Trio, flown in from Little Rock especially for the party. Elaborate flower arrangements of orchids, bird of paradise, and other blossoms from all over the world were created by Hal Cunningham. The guest list included Cesar Romero, Suzanne Pleshette, Anne Baxter, Anne Francis, Maria Cole (widow of Nat King Cole and mother of Natalie Cole), Marion (Mrs. Francis) Lederer, "alumna" Marilyn Maxwell, and many others. Joan Crawford was unable to attend due to her hectic schedule running Pepsi-Cola in New York City (see letters pages 104–105). The kickoff party took place on June 22, 1969. The event's $100.00 per ticket proceeds went to a local charity. Esplanade remained open until 1973 and was the frequent site of weddings, charity events, and timely art shows (see plates 192–195; guests).

JOAN CRAWFORD

September 7, 1969

Sascha dear,

I received the Esplanade "circular" and it is very interesting. It must be a fabulous showroom-gallery, and I hope to shop there when I am in southern California again. Thank you for mentioning me in your advertisement, and you are so right, dear friend, you are indeed a favorite jeweler of mine, and a favorite friend as well.

Bless you, and my fond wishes to you and Bill.

Joan

Christmas, 1969

Sascha dear,

    These greetings are sent with my deep gratitude for your friendship. May you enjoy happiness, and may you and your loved ones always be at peace with God.

JOAN CRAWFORD

September 7, 1969

Bill dear,

Thank you so very much for seeing that I received an announcement of the opening of Esplanade in Santa Monica. It sounds like a fantastic place, and I am so looking forward to shopping there when I go to California again. Your antiques, reproductions, accessories and custom finishing must be so exciting.

Bless you, and my love to you and your mother - and to Sascha too.

    As ever,

Plate 192: Esplanade opening. Left to right: Film star Cesar Romero, film director George Seaton, Beverly Hills mayor Phyllis Seaton, and author Bill Seay.

Plate 193: Esplanade opening. Howard Shoup discusses design with Suzanne Pleshette.

Plate 194: Esplanade opening. Anne Baxter talks with author Bill Seay.

Plate 195: Esplanade opening. Marilyn Maxwell and Sascha. They discuss his former show at the Dalzell Hatfield Gallery.

The January 25, 1970, issue of the *Los Angeles Times* Home magazine unveiled yet another Brastoff brainchild: "Living Art" — the shaping, carving, and tooling of Styrofoam and plastic. Sascha chose Styrofoam because it was inexpensive, easily carved and very durable if given reasonable care. He would either hand carve the material or use an electric wood burning tool, like we used at summer camp! The finished pieces could then be coated in a variety of waterproof spray paints. He also used a kind of "cold liquid metal" that he developed. He purportedly was offered a large sum to sell its formula to a chemical or manufacturing company. Sascha never revealed this secret process and took the information to his grave. Referring to this new art form as "Hortisculpture", Sascha filled them with easy to grow succulents and bromeliads. They have small root systems and require little water. He was also quite fond of their color and texture. Sascha offered these pieces for sale at Esplanade and, after his passing, we found many in his backyard studio and garden. We have never seen them for sale before; whether in an antique mall, swap meet or even at yard sales. All of them had Sascha's name (in some version) carved underneath. S.B. was negotiating with a New York manufacturer

Plate 196: "Rooftops" in Styrofoam.

about mass producing a machine moulded version of these originals but the idea never got off the ground. (See plates 196–201; Polaroids taken by Sascha in his backyard. Also, plates 202 & 203; hand carved Styrofoam "wall" commissioned by Dow Chemical for their Los Angeles office.)

Plate 197: Abstract design.

Plate 198: A very delicate Styrofoam-wreath supports flower pot.

Plate 199: Assorted hand carved,
Styrofoam flower pots.

Plate 200: Carved and metal plated pot.

Plate 202: Two panels of the Styrofoam wall.

Plate 201: A fantastic, heavily carved
Styrofoam wig head!

Plate 203: Sascha working on the
Styrofoam wall.

By the early 1970s, Sascha had a complete change of philosophy regarding the creation and integrity of his artwork. During his prolific 35 year career, Sascha excelled in classical dance, show business, costume design, ceramics, metal sculpture, jewelry, enamel work, oil painting, public commissions, multi-media sketching, and was a pioneer in many production techniques. Sascha had always maintained total control over the creation, mass production, and marketing of his "style." In a 1963 letter, he expressed a desire to "find some agent or someone who would know how to utilize the 'Sascha Brastoff' name & personality & perhaps use it on many different things; fabrics, clothes, etc." Almost ten years later, he decided to "sell" his name, or merchandise it, to virtually anyone who made a reasonable offer. Many of these deals were quite lucrative, though we feel some compromises were made. Without printing a laundry list of these alliances, we'll give you those we feel are important for any collector to know.

Plate 204: Ad slick for Haegar pottery

Plate 205: Catalog for Haeger's "Sascha" collection.

The 1971 "Centennial Edition" catalog for the Haeger Pottery of Dundee, Illinois, featured two ceramic lines bearing a mold impressed "Sascha B" – "Esplanade" and "Roman Bronze." These pieces, in a grayish/brownish green with metallic overlay, were perfect for the dark wood, Spanish/Mediterranean look of the '70s. Other versions were produced in white and gold (see plates 204 & 205).

In 1972, Sascha started to produce a line of costume jewelry called "Sascha Brastoff Designs." Marilyn Watson formed a company to market these designs at gift shows in 1973. The joint venture yielded "Sascha Brastoff Designs/For Marilyn Watson Creations", with offices at 9956 Santa Monica Boulevard in Beverly Hills. They also had a showroom in downtown L.A.'s jewelry district. Miss Watson represented Sascha's fine jewelry and miniature gold plated sculptures, and arranged for specially commissioned work. Sascha's jewelry was predominately nature and animal themed, although he also made reverent, zodiac, "nugget," and novelty pieces. A controversial pendant combining a cross, the Star of David, and an ankh symbolized Sascha's belief in a universal religion. The nugget and costume lines were made of jeweler's metal that was 24K gold electroplated. They were priced in 1973 at $5.00 – $30.00 retail. The miniature sculptures were cast using the lost wax process in bronze and then gold electroplated. A finished piece was mounted on an Italian marble base with a brass signature plate. The delicate "Ming Tree" was top of the line and sold for $150.00. The following year it was offered in retail stores at $200.00! Sascha's vermeil jewelry (gold plated sterling silver) and 14K creations retailed from $200.00 to $2,000.00. Miss Watson believed "the return of elegance is a fashion fact and a strong factor in the increasing appreciation of Brastoff's jewelry." By 1974 they added several new lines composed of sterling silver ("Fabrics of the Sea"), natural geode, lucite, porcelain, and stoneware (not pictured; see plates 206 & 207).

Plate 206: Gold zodiac necklace.

Plate 207: Marilyn Watson wearing a Sascha creation.

In 1973, Sascha marketed a series of his classic animal designs with the Marina Metal Arts company of Marina del Rey, California. Sascha initially created these images on scratchboard (black "chalkboard" over stark white) with dramatic results. The finished items were then printed on either gold or silver foil in exact duplicates and reversals of each design (see plate 208 and consult Price Guide pages 221 & 222 for original chalkboards). They were also etched or pressed, on a limited basis, into different types of metal — copper, brass and white metal and enamel over copper. Sascha's agreement with MMA included "an exclusive license to manufacture and sell costume jewelry (not gold) and certain miniature sculpture." See Price Guide pages 148, 184 & 208 for these metal pieces.

Plate 208: Assorted scratchboard originals printed on foil.

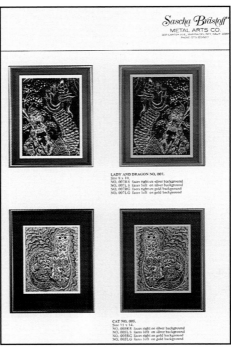

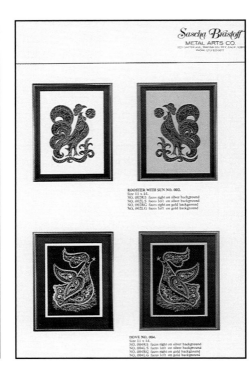

A circa 1975 collaboration with Merle Norman Cosmetics on a selection of pins and pendants included a "fragrant fashion accessory designed for Merle Norman by Sascha Brastoff." This was a gold plated lion's head pendant available in 3 different scents! Weren't we all fashion victims back in the '70s?! (See plates 209 & 210.)

Arguably the best co-venture was the 1976 Silver Circus issued by the Franklin Mint of Franklin Center, Pennsylvania. The Silver Circus was a limited edition set of six sculptures available exclusively to established Franklin Mint collectors. The series contained "The Performing Seal", "The Clown", "The Butterfly Girl", "The Dancing Horse", "The Ringmaster," and "The Circus Lion". It took Sascha one year to create the final wax prototypes, which were then made in solid sterling silver accented with pure 24 karat gold. They were offered at the rate of one every 3 months and cost $240.00 per sculpture. Payment arrangements could be made at $80.00 per month bringing the total cost of the set to $1,440.00! A certificate of quality and authenticity was also issued. The limited offer expired on October 25, 1976. Steve Conti called the Franklin Mint for the exact number of sets produced and sold. They claimed to have no record of this information due to the age of the Silver Circus. See page 235; this set, belonging to A. DeWayne Bethany, was photographed in front of Sascha's original drawings used to create the series.

Fragrance in the Form of Exquisite Fine Jewelry

The Fragrance Pendant Necklace

Ensemble of midnight lace with ruffle-edged peignoir over pinafore-topped gown, from the Merle Norman Collection . . . $40.00.

This ornate golden lion's head holds a ceramic tile impregnated with fragrance. A beautiful fashion accessory . . . a unique fragrance accessory. A Merle Norman exclusive designed by famed artist and ceramist Sascha Brastoff. Fragrance Pendant, complete with gold plated chain, and fragrance tile in Kari, Baroque or MN . . . $10.00.

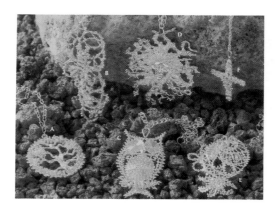

Plate 209: Costume jewelry designed for Merle Norman. A. Ming Tree. B. Abstract. C. Owl. D. Zodiac. E. Fish. F. Cross.

Plate 210: A "fragrant" error by Sascha!

Also in 1976, Sascha experimented with the country living market with rustic, hand thrown pottery planters and vases. These are extremely rare and look much like typical 1970s studio pottery, but better, of course! All had sgraffito signatures and some were dated (see plates 211 & 212; Polaroids taken by Sascha).

Plate 211: A Sascha original stoneware flower pot.

Plate 212: Sascha's hand thrown pottery.

"American Bisque Porcelains, Inc. cordially invites you to the premiere"...etc., etc., etc. Still another marketing deal to produce pieces that were partly re-issues of earlier Brastoff designs (like the "Aztec Cat", originally one of S.B.'s mosaic series) and partly new ideas. Favorite among collectors and somewhat prized for their scarcity are the "Peek and Boo Polar Bears" (see original catalog photos; plates 213–215 and page 233). All ABP pieces were marked with a black factory decal of the Liberty Bell and a separate decal bearing "Sascha Brastoff" written in script. The line debuted in July 1977.

A kickoff party on December 6, 1977, celebrated an exclusive agreement with California Jewelsmiths, Inc. of Beverly Hills. "The Sascha Brastoff Galleria", located upstairs in the posh jewelry store, sold his finest 14K gold and precious stone jewelry. Select examples of oil paintings, metal sculpture, enamels, and other specialty items were also retailed. Artware produced by the Marina Metal Arts and American Bisque Porcelains companies were among the offerings. Sascha based out of this store for all of his custom jewelry orders. His client list again included Jeannette Rockefeller, Eva Gabor, Lucille Ball, and other celebrities (see original fine jewelry photos; plates 216 – 221). The most innovative creation was Sascha's "Living Sculpture"; heavy 14K gold and jewel encrusted decorative items with detachable parts that could be worn as a pin, pendant, or brooch. One piece, depicting a scallop shell held up by three seahorses, adorned with cabochon emeralds and rubies, has a diamond studded mermaid perched on top. The mermaid is the detachable pendant! See plate 222 — a Living Sculpture offered at the opening for $10,000!

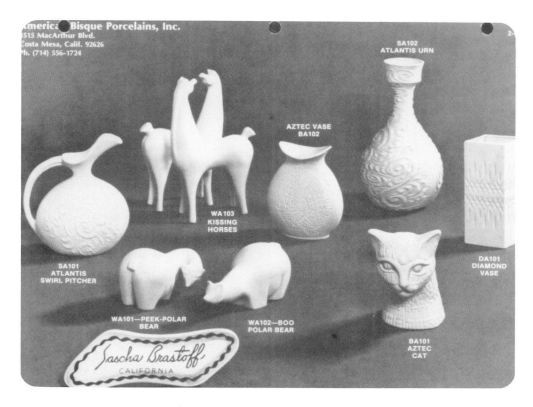

Plate 213: "ABP" catalog circa 1977.

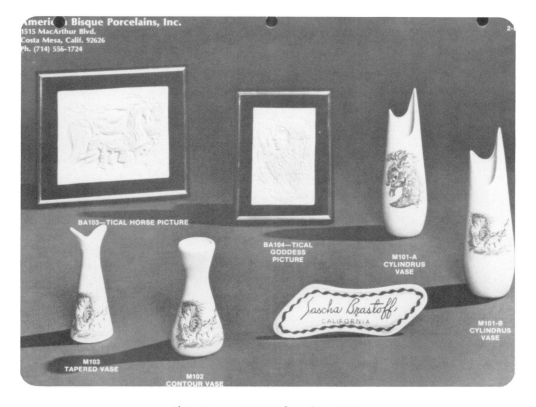

Plate 214: "ABP" catalog circa 1977.

erica Bisque Porcelains, Inc.
15 MacArthur Blvd.
osta Mesa, Calif. 92626
(714) 556-1724

1-F

SA104
ATLANTIS SUNBURST
LIMITED EDITION OF 500

BA103 THE AZTEC HORSE

Sascha Brastoff,
CALIFORNIA

SA103
ATLANTIS WOMAN
PITCHER

Plate 215: "ABP" catalog circa 1977.

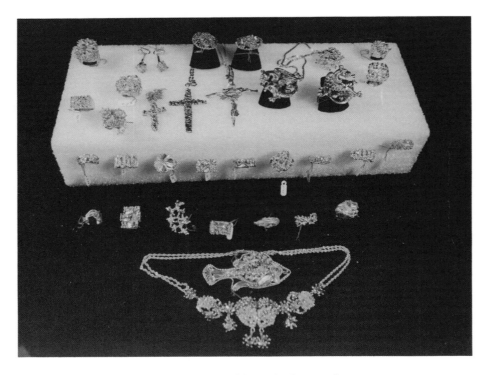

Plate 216: Fine gold jewelry by Sascha.

Plate 217: Assorted gold and precious stone jewelry and a
miniature sculpture, "The Mask", by Sascha.

Plate 218: An 18K gold bird with tiny diamonds and a huge pearl body. By Sascha.

Plate 219: A gold peacock pin covered with diamonds and emeralds, by Sascha.

Plate 220: 18K gold dragonfly pin with diamonds, opals, coral, and turquoise on a succulent plant in Sascha's garden.

Plate 221: A black opal mounted in a gold ring with crude emeralds, sapphires and diamonds by Sascha.

Plate 222: "Sea Goddess," 6" high.
Made from 14 ounces of 14k gold, with rubies, emeralds, and diamonds.
The mermaid is actually a pendant!
Courtesy of the Borens and an anonymous California collector.

January of 1979 saw the release of an individually numbered, 7,500 edition series of plates titled "Flower Bouquet." The original design was created exclusively for a walk-in fireplace at the Rockefeller estate, *Winrock* in Arkansas. "#0001" of the series was presented to Mrs. Winthrop Rockefeller. Each multi-produced piece had very fine, hand applied gold work. The translucent china plates were made by California Porcelain & Bronze Inc. of Glendora, California, and priced at $65.00 each. It is unknown how many of the intended 7,500 were ever produced or actually sold (see plate 223).

Sascha released a line of brass plated "Wall Sculpture Switch Plates" from 1977 through 1979. Produced and marketed by the Melard Manufacturing Corporation of Passaic, New Jersey, these unique decorator items were shipped to small, independently owned hardware stores specializing in basic home repair and gardening supplies. The elaborate items retailed for $35.00 – $50.00 each and, unfortunately for Sascha, were displayed in the same sections as their 49¢ plastic counterparts! (See plate 224 and page 148)

Plate 223: "Flower Bouquet" circa 1979.

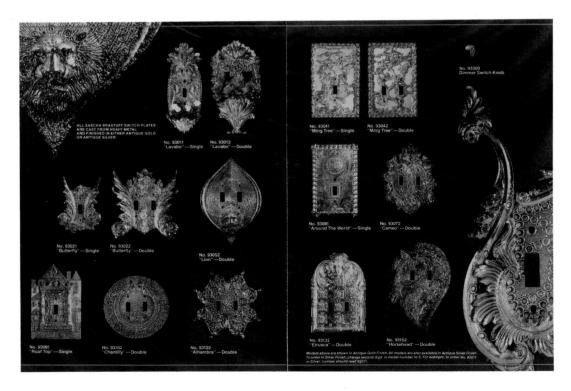

Plate 224: Sascha's high, rococco-style light switch plates never really had an audience.

120

Sascha had a most pleasant collaboration with the Melard people and, apparently, trusted their judgment and ability to market the Brastoff name. His deal with Melard included the production and sale of Styrofoam tiles for both wall and acoustical ceiling use, lithographs, lucite paperweights with metal imbedments, and a line of bathroom fittings & fixtures, to name just a few. We don't know how many of these items were actually produced or ever got to retail outlets, but Melard certainly had big plans for Sascha.

We gave the Best Technical Achievement Award to Sascha's "Space Age Hologram Jewelry", first marketed in 1979. Holography is the technique of using laser beams to produce a three-dimensional image of an object. The theory behind holograms was developed in 1947 by scientist Dennis Gabor. The technique was further improved in 1961 with the creation of the laser (Light Amplification by Stimulated Emission of Radiation). The light projected from a laser is unvarying in frequency and permits clarity and sharpness of the image. As early as 1977, holography became another creative tool for Sascha. Specially coated light sensitive glass, imported from Sweden, was exposed, developed, cut, sealed, and finished entirely by hand. The completed hologram is easily viewed with any single, direct light source — sunlight, moonlight, even flashlight! Sascha used his original gold jewelry and sculpture for his holograms —

Plate 225: Hologram ad;
Los Angeles magazine, 1979.

astrological symbols, religious and animal motifs. Circular pendants were 1¾" in diameter and mounted in gold finished or plated bezels. Larger square and rectangular ones were for single or multi-frame display. Sascha felt the colors in his holograms were "matched in nature only by the opal." S.B.'s holograms were produced by Hummelwerk; a division of Goebel Art Inc., Rodental, West Germany, and imported to the states through their Elmsford, New York, office. They retailed at $40.00 each and were available at fine jewelry, gift, and department stores. Like all holograms, Sascha's were only appreciated by a small group of collectors and are hard to find today (see plate 225 and Price Guide page 210 & 211). Hummelwerk also produced a "Star Steed" decorative plate made from fine jeweler's bronze, electroplated with 24K gold and offered for $125.00, retail.

Film veteran Henry Fonda was presented with the American National Theatre and Academy (west coast faction) or ANTA award on January 1, 1980, in

Denver, Colorado. ANTA, founded by Congress in 1935, had given its premiere award to the first family of the American theatre, Alfred Lunt and Lynn Fontanne, in 1972 for their golden wedding anniversary. The award medallions presented to the Lunts and to Fonda were hand sculpted in heavy gold by Sascha. Each piece was personalized, signed and dated. "Talk about a collector's item!" Sascha quipped to ANTA's first president, Francis Lederer, who com-

Plate 226: Face side; ANTA award.

Plate 227: Original Sascha "art photo" of Fred Astaire's 1978 ANTA award.

missioned Sascha to create the $2,100.00 jewel. The list of recipients of the ANTA award medallion includes Fred Astaire (1978), Helen Hayes, Bob Hope (1981), Rosalind Russell, and Katharine Cornell. ANTA's honorary chairperson was Betty Ford (see plates 226 & 227).

Actor Michael Landon commissioned Sascha to create a very special "Holocaust Star" to give to producers, directors, and other Hollywood peers. The 2" x 2" medallion in heavily gold plated jeweler's bronze depicted a Star of David formed out of barbed wire with a hand reaching up from the underside of the star. The clenched fist is grasping and breaking the central part of barbed wire — symbolizing the abolition of worldwide anti-Semitism. Author Steve Conti purchased Sascha's personal "Holocaust Star" (the only one found in S.B.'s estate) and donated it to The Museum of Tolerance in Los Angeles' Simon Wiesenthal Center. The controversial and emotionally moving piece is part of the permanent archives of the museum. A holographic pendant was also made of this image (see plate 228).

Plate 228: Holocaust Star.

In doing the research for this book, Steve Conti interviewed an engineer with the development company that bought Sascha's West Olympic Boulevard factory in 1981. The engineer told him that the building had been a Chrysler dealership for several years prior to closing sometime in 1979 or 1980. The site was purchased primarily for the land and, within one month of the building's demolition in 1981, construction was started on a multi-story office complex. Since 1983 Olympic Plaza, as it is called today, has been the home of City National Bank and several law and medical businesses. When asked if any relics were saved from the Brastoff factory; i.e. wrought iron, the front signage, etc., the engineer replied, "it's all become landfill somewhere in San Bernardino County."

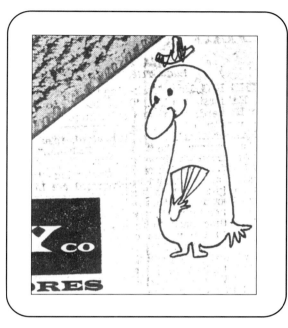

By the mid '80s, Sascha's craft had come full circle to his roots at the Clay Club in New York City and his "Whimsies." He created a series of contemporary line drawings with a variety of themes — social commentary, typical American family life, even retrospection to his younger days. He finally seemed satisfied with himself and his lifelong accomplishments (see plates 229 & 230).

Plate 229: Sketches by Sascha as found on notepads and slips of paper in home.

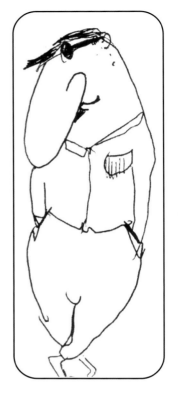

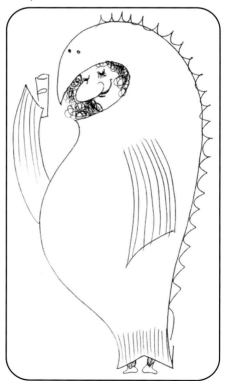

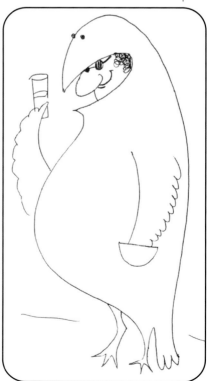

Plate 230: Sketches by Sascha.

The 1980s also brought a fierce battle against prostate cancer, a leading cause of death for adult males. Sascha spent the last several years of his life visiting with friend Filomena Bruno. Filomena was "sent by God," said Sascha, and saw to it that all of his daily needs were met. Filomena Bruno and Howard Shoup were regular participants in Sascha's Thursday night poker games. Shoup's death on May 29, 1987, came as a crushing blow to Sascha. After losing this friend of 45 years, Sascha lost his zest for living. His desire to create things of beauty would never return (see plate 231 – last photo taken of Sascha and Howard together).

In 1989, Sascha was attacked and brutally beaten while gardening in front of his home, by an assailant later proven to be under the influence of drugs. Sascha was badly injured and had to be hospitalized. He never fully recovered from the senseless, unprovoked attack. Bill Seay recalls encouraging Sascha to start drawing again, at least for his own enjoyment. A tearful Sascha remarked, "Bill, my friend, I'm all drawn out."

During Sascha's valiant bout with cancer, he never ignored public attention. Seldom venturing out due to the intense discomfort and pain, Sascha spent most of his days with Filomena Bruno and his beloved dog, Rocky. DeWayne Bethany had a large garden party the summer before Sascha's death. Of course Sascha was invited and, of course, he at first refused. Bill Seay finally convinced him that a couple of hours with old friends would be good for him. Upon Sascha's arrival, he heard a fabulous musician playing and the party guests enjoying food, drink, and good conversation. Within moments the word spread that Sascha was present and soon a large group gathered around him. With his ribald jokes, impersonations, and highly infec-

Plate 231: Sascha Brastoff and Howard Shoup with *Winged Victory* memorabilia.

tious laughter, Sascha had a captive audience. For several hours he continued the "act" and really enjoyed himself. Finally, an exhausted Sascha asked Bill to drive him home. Sadly, the party guests said goodnight. This was Sascha's last public appearance.

Sascha passed away on February 4, 1993, at the age of 74. He is survived by his beloved sister Evelyn, various family members and the millions of ardent fans touched by his unique sense of style, humor, and limitless artistic talent.

It was our mission to publish this book as a loving tribute to this Renaissance man who for the last 10 years of his prolific 50 year career was misunderstood, misquoted and misrepresented as "that ceramics guy — the man who decorated ashtrays". Bill Seay remarked, "Sascha was a true genius... he could work on an intricate sketch, tell a staff artist what to paint, entertain a visiting customer and think of a new jewelry design... all the while tapping his foot to music." Sascha and Bill were the best of friends and we (Bethany and Conti) consider Bill the foremost authority on Sascha's life and work. Sascha left behind a bountiful legacy of artwork for all the world to enjoy. We believe we have dispelled all of this misinformation and, hopefully, have set the record straight.

Plate 232: Sascha Brastoff as he will always be remembered.

⚜ *Chapter 4* ⚜
What's in a Name?

When determining whether a piece was hand decorated by Sascha or commercially mass produced, the collector must understand that Sascha was to the art world what Liberace was to a piano, Dagmar to show biz, Fabian to '60s rock & roll, and Twiggy to modeling. Sascha Brastoff was known to his show business friends, personal clients, and the masses simply as Sascha or Sascha B. He didn't need to use a last name, although fully signed pieces were obviously done by S.B. himself.

We divided his biography into 3 distinct chapters to easily illustrate his signature and/or marking system. Pieces produced as early as 1940 at the Clay Club in New York City were signed "Sascha" or in full. War bond posters & sketches done during World War II were signed "Sascha", Pvt. (Private) or Sgt. (Sergeant) Brastoff (see plates 21 & 22 in Chapter I). Costume designs done at 20th Century Fox during 1946 – 47 were also signed "Sascha" (see plates 325–331 in Price Guide section). When Sascha entered into commercial ceramic production with his first factory in 1947 and employed other artists to hand decorate his designs, "Sascha B" became the standard signature; usually front lower right or left. No underside mark or logo appears on these ceramics (see Price Guide section for "early" production pieces).

With the opening of Sascha's new studio-factory on November 18, 1953, the chanticleer, or rooster, logo was used on the underside of all commercially produced items and some of Sascha's personal creations. A gold "machine" signature, or stamp, identified each piece as "Sascha Brastoff CALIFORNIA U.S.A. ©". A hand written style number also appeared under this stamp (see plate 233). The name "Sascha B", hand written by a staff decorator, can be found on the front or topside of the piece.

When Sascha left his factory sometime in 1962, a hand written registered trademark symbol "®" appeared with "Sascha B" and a style number (see plate 234). This signature can be found on the topside of a piece with or without an underside rooster. It can also be found solely on the underside; as pictured. This was used until sometime in 1973 when all commercial production from this factory ceased. According to Filomena Bruno, decorative items were also purchased from gift and trade shows in an attempt to increase the failing company's sales and profits. These

Plate 233: Commercial mark post 1953.

Plate 234: Commercial mark post 1962.

pieces were "signed" (with an etched "Sascha B" and "®") or marked with a paper label. The highly prized "Resin" (or Resolite; Jacquelite) animal series were amongst these procured items. Resin votive candleholders were manufactured by Continental Candle Co., Inc. in Northridge, California. Some resin items have the copyright symbol ("©"), instead of the registered trademark symbol, in conjunction with Sascha's name. Mr. Bethany spoke to one collector who has a resin animal with a full (etched) signature and date "1969". The gentleman spoke to Sascha sometime in the early '90s and asked him whether or not he created the piece. Sascha replied, "I don't know who signed it, but it wasn't Sascha Brastoff!"

All personally created/decorated ceramic pieces carried a full signature and were occasionally dated. This encompasses Sascha's entire career (see Price Guide section for specific examples). All of his drawings were signed "Sascha", "Sascha B", or in full and sometimes dated. At no time were staff decorators at any factory allowed to produce sketches or drawings for retail.

As stated in Chapter 2, Sascha *preferred* to work in the same room with his staff artists. Some items decorated by Sascha himself while on the main floor were signed "Sascha B." It is important to note that some inexpensively offered commercial pieces were actually done by Sascha. After inspecting hundreds of them, we can usually determine if a post 1947 or 1953 "Sascha B" piece was done by the master himself. Please remember that there is a one in four chance of finding S.B.'s handiwork if the item was produced the late '40s, when Sascha had 3 other decorators working with him. There is a one in 40 chance of this if the piece was produced between 1953 and 1962, when Sascha's decorator staff fluctuated between 40 and 50 according to our research. Post 1962 factory pieces were only staff decorated. We've also pointed out that Sascha's gold application was finer and thinner than any his artists could do. This is a direct giveaway on many of the "Sascha B" signed ceramics, especially the "Persian" and "Star Steed " lines (see pages 162 & 163; 199 – 201 in the Collector's Price Guide section).

Sascha's metal sculpture and miniature, gold plated sculpture bore a brass or gold plated signature plate affixed to a base which was usually of marble or wood. Some of the larger welded steel sculpture had a scratched signature in some configuration. As is the case with any artist, there are unsigned examples, too, (although rare).

All of Sascha's marked jewelry had an impressed or scratched "Sascha", "Sascha B", or a full signature and sometimes a date.

Here is a selection of original signatures carved into black scratchboard circa mid 1970s (see plate 235).

Plate 235: Assorted scratchboard signatures, circa 1975.

When Sascha produced artwork out of his home studio, he frequently affixed a gold metallic paper label to it, whether signed or unsigned. These labels stated either "A Special Elegance by Sascha Brastoff" or "Sascha Brastoff Designs Inc." (see plate 236.)

Please refer to Chapter III for a description of joint ventures or merchandise deals and their respective markings.

We hope that by now you are informed and enlightened... and not too confused.

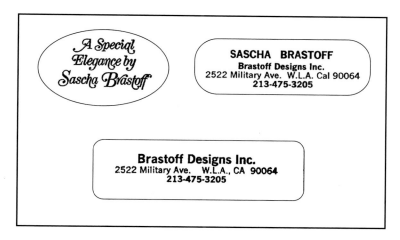

Plate 236: A sampling of Sascha's "home studio" labels.

Here is a recap:

	"Sascha"	"Sascha B"	"Sascha Brastoff"
1940 – 1945	X		X
1946 – 1947	X		X
(11/18) 1947 – 1953	X	X	X
(11/18) (4/3) 1953 – 1962	X	Rooster Logo X	X
1962 – 1973 Factory w/o Sascha		X ® occasionally ©	
1962 – mid 1980s Sascha Brastoff Designs	X	X	X
mid 1980s – 1993	NO WORK GENERATED DUE TO POOR HEALTH		

It's important to note there are always items inconsistent with established marking procedures in any vein of mass production. We feel you're now equipped with the basics to make a logical assessment on the age and authenticity of a "Sascha" piece.

Of all the talented artists and decorators that worked for Sascha, two should be singled out for their individual style.

Matthew Adams exclusively painted all of Sascha's "Alaska" ceramic line. These pieces were originally designed by Sascha for the Juneau, Alaska, tourist market. After delivery from the southern California factory, a paper label declaring "Souvenir of Alaska" was affixed. Ironically, many were purchased by California tourists and brought right back to the Southland! Upon leaving Brastoff's company, Matt Adams was granted permission to continue producing "Alaska" pieces. These are signed "Matthew Adams" or "Matt Adams" (see plate 441 in Price Guide section).

Marc Bellaire was another Brastoff protegé. His style was noticeably influenced by Sascha, and when he left the company, became even more flamboyant. His "Friendly Island" series of dancing natives and festive "Mardi Gras" designs were typical of 1950s camp decor. One large ashtray is a direct knock-off of Sascha's "Chi Chi Bird" design (see plates 445 and 446 in Price Guide section). All were signed either "Marc Bellaire" or "Bellaire."

Sascha's success influenced other manufacturers to copy his designs, both domestically and overseas. (See plate 444 in Price Guide section). The Homer Laughlin China Co. produced a typical, provincial rooster plate in 1953. Homer Laughlin had its most successful run against Bauer Pottery's brightly colored dinnerware with its Fiesta line. Also pictured in this group is a bowl from Eddie Kourishima's Venice Clay Shops, circa 1963. Kourishima had been artistic director at the Brastoff plant. The tall "Sarena" vase is presumed to have been done at the Venice Clay Shops. The free form "Pagoda" ashtray was actually made by the Enesco Company of Japan, noted for their collectible head vases; highly prized today. The "Surf Ballet" knock-off pipe was probably produced by Santa Anita Ware of California.

❧ Collector's Price Guide ❧

All of our price determinations were based solely upon the market here in Los Angeles, where the bulk of our pieces were bought. All prices are for items in excellent original condition; all others are noted. Prices for items purchased from Sascha's estate reflect the current market value at the time of publishing, whether higher or lower than what they actually transacted for. Sascha's personal collection is denoted as "estate" throughout the Price Guide. In certain instances we may feel an item is truly irreplaceable or of such sentimental value, we chose not to assess a price. Those pieces are noted as "NPA" (No Price Available) or "NFS" (Not For Sale). The author's feel it is "art for art's sake". If you find a particular piece exciting and wonderful, you should be prepared to pay a little more for it. You can't always go by what ANY book says; you must always follow your heart.

Please refer to Chapter 4 for details on Sascha's marking system. For the ease and clarity of this price guide, all pieces were produced at the West Olympic Boulevard studio-factory after 1953 and prior to 1962 using the rooster logo. All other pieces are denoted as "early" (produced from 1947 to 1952) or "post factory" (made from 1962 to approximately 1973 using Sascha's name in his absence). Fully signed and/or dated items are noted.

THE A. DEWAYNE BETHANY COLLECTION

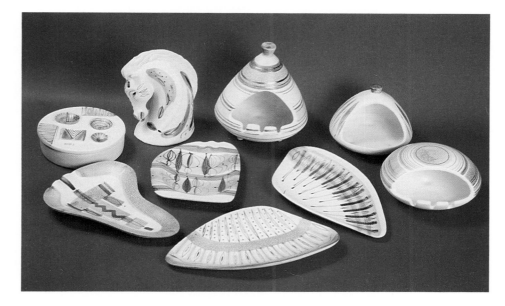

Plate 237: ABSTRACT (clockwise from top left)

Covered box with unusual impressed lid, style CB23, 5", $90.00

Horse head, style S9, 5¾" (no base), $125.00

Hooded ashtray, style H6, 7", $55.00

Hooded ashtray, style H13, 4½", $45.00

Hooded ashtray, style H1, 3", $45.00

Free form dish, style F3, 10", $35.00

Free form dish, style F3, 10", $20.00 (rim chip)

Free form ashtray, style F2, 8", $30.00

Free form ashtray, style F1, 6½", $40.00 (center piece)

Plate 238: ABSTRACT (clockwise from top left)

Free form ashtray, style F8, 17", $160.00

Vase, style L5, 6", $35.00

Candy dish with lid, style O96, 10", $135.00

Shell dish, style S24, 12", $80.00 (rim chip)

Shell dish, style S52, 12", $65.00 (rim chip)

Covered box, style O20, 5", $60.00

Lighter, style L1, 3", $45.00

Vase, style L2, 5", $35.00

Rectangular covered box, style O24, 7", $65.00

(Note: Vases in "L" styles were actually lighter bases factory purchased without flame apparatus)

Plate 239: ABSTRACT (clockwise from top left)

Ashtray, style O8, 12", $75.00

Chop plate, style O53, 17", $175.00 (no factory mark or signature)

Vase, style O84, 17", $100.00

Rectangular covered box, style O25, 10½", $80.00

Square ashtray, style O3B, 8", $35.00 (chip)

Piggy bank, style S14, 5", $95.00

Square ashtray, style O3, 5", $45.00

Free form dish, style C3, 7", $45.00

Square dish, style O6, 8", $60.00

Covered box, style O20, 5", $60.00 (center piece)

Plate 240: ABSTRACT (clockwise from top left)

Ashtray, style O7, 10", $60.00

Divided plate, style D55, 12", $95.00 (part of "Rondo" Buffet Service)

Free form plate, style F42, 10", $75.00

Ashtray, no style number, 6½", $250.00 (fully signed on back; collection of Bill Seay)

Square dish, style O6, 8", $60.00

Square dish, style O6, 8", $60.00

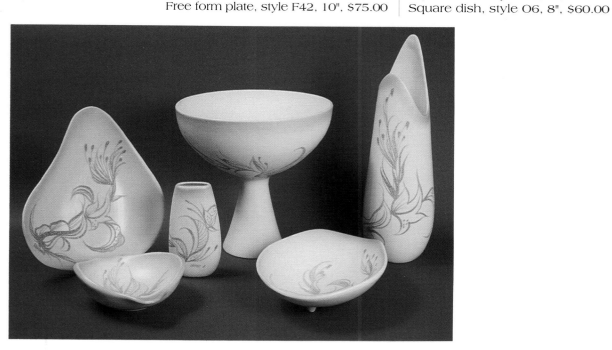

Plate 241: MISTY BLUE (clockwise from top left)

Free form bowl, style F40, 10", $55–$65

Vase, style L4, 6", $40–$50 (lighter base purchased as vase)

Fruit bowl, style O61, 11", $175.00

Free form vase, style O94, 13½", $90–$100

Footed bowl, style C4, 9", $55–$65

Nut dish, style C2, 7", $35–$45

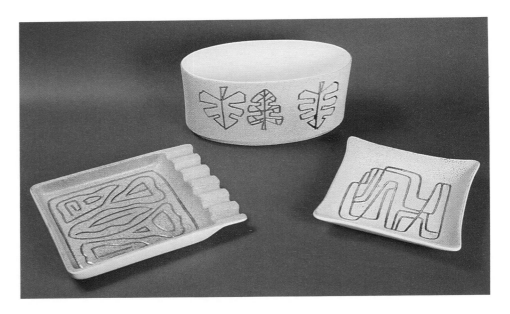

Plate 242: CELADON (l to r)
Ashtray, style O7, 10", $95.00
Ovoid planter, style O30, 10", $125.00 | Square dish, style O6, 8", $75.00

Plate 243: JEWEL BIRD (clockwise from top left)
Coffee pot, style O71, 15",
  $200.00
Egg, style O44B, 10", $125.00
Vase, style O42, 9", $75.00
Vase, style F20, 5", $40–$50 | Free form ashtray, style F1, 7",
  $30.00
Free form box, style F1B, 7",
  $65–$75
Tankard, style O70, 5", $40–$50

Plate 244: JEWEL BIRD (clockwise from top left)

Candlestick, style O83B, 8", $50.00

Chop plate, style O52, 15", $150.00

Hooded ashtray, style H3, 4½", $65–75

(Peacock pattern; only one found)

Square dish, style O5, 8", $50.00

Nut dishes (3), style O1, 2½", $20 each

Plate 245: MINOS (clockwise from top left)

Ashtray, style O8, 12", $85.00

Free form bowl, style O93, 10", $165.00

Footed bowl, style C4, 9", $75.00

Footed bowl, style C4, 9", $75.00

Elliptical box, style O22, 7", $110.00

(marked incorrectly as O26)

Ashtray, style O8A, 8", $30.00 (underside chip)

(Note: None of these are early pieces and do not have a factory rooster mark)

Plate 246: ROOFTOPS (clockwise from top left)

Pitcher, no style number, 11",
   $185.00

Free form dish, style F42, 10",
   $65.00

Free form ashtray ("bigfoot"),
   style F2, 8", $25.00 (rim chip)

Covered box, style O21, 8",
   $85–$100

Cigarette holder, style L1, 3",
   $20.00 (rim flakes)

Square dish, style O6, 8",
   $50.00

Plate 247: ROOFTOPS

Tea canister, style C43,
   13", $250.00

Tea canister, no style

number, 10½", $200.00

Boomerang box, style F5B,
   12", $175.00

Plate 248: ROOFTOPS (clockwise from top left)
Free form dish, style F42, 10",
   $65.00
Plate, style O50, 10", $75.00

Square dish, style O6, 8", $55.00
Round box, style O23, 5", $75.00

THE FOLLOWING SASCHA ORIGINALS ARE FROM
THE A. DEWAYNE BETHANY COLLECTION

Plate 249: LUCITE EGGS (l to r)
9" x 6", hand tooled and flowered
   with "LOVE" on one side, signed
   Sascha '72, 1 of 4 known produced, $600.00
9" x 6", hand tooled and flowered,
   signed Sascha '72, 1 of 4 known

produced, $600.00
9" x 6", hand tooled, "Night and Day,"
   signed Sascha '72, 1 of 4 known
   produced, $600.00
(All of the above were purchased
   from Sascha's estate)

Plate 250:
10" x 12", watercolor depicting wartime ruins in Bremen, Germany, signed '45 Sascha, $450.00, estate

Plate 251:
10" x 12", watercolor of two angels; Bremen, Germany, signed Sascha '45, $450.00, estate

Plate 252:
7" ovoid dish, sgraffito detail of masked acrobat, copper/plat-
inum wash, with top and underside signatures and date,
$1,250.00, estate

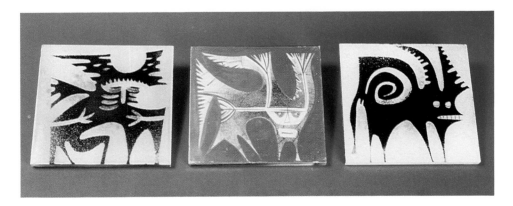

Plate 253:
6" x 6" tiles (set of 3), abstract animals, unsigned, with paper labels,
$900.00, estate (possibly extra tiles from Sascha's home studio shower)

Plate 254:
9" ashtray, puff glaze of leaves on
green ground, full signature,
$650.00

Plate 255:
9" dish, sgraffito leaves on
dark green/brown ground,
full signature/'62 on front,
$550.00

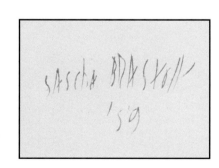

Plate 256:
8" plate, alien amphibious creature in very fine gold work, with underside signature and
date, $900.00 (rim chip)

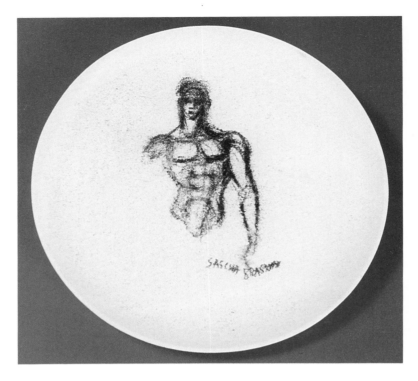

Plate 257:
10" plate, male anatomical study in cobalt on cream ground, full signature, 2 factory flaws, $950.00

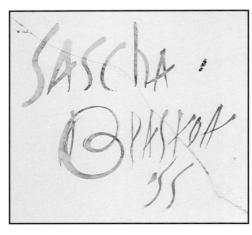

Plate 258:
11½" fish shaped plate, marine life in gold on blue faux raku ground, with underside signature, broken in '94 L.A. earthquake, $500.00

Plate 259:
10" plate, "Minos" pattern, raised figure in pewter tone, obscured full signature on front, $550.00, estate

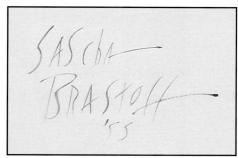

Plate 260:
12" plate, slip decorated flowers arranged in bowl, very fine gold detail, with underside signature and date, $900.00

Plate 261:
13" free form bowl, style F43, "Rooftops" pattern, personalized to film star Marilyn Maxwell (for opening of West Los Angeles studio-factory, signed and dated 1953), $750.00

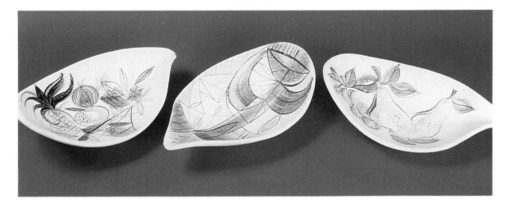

Plate 262:
9" free form bowls, set of 3, from former employee of Brastoff factory, full signature underside 1 bowl, $900.00 for set

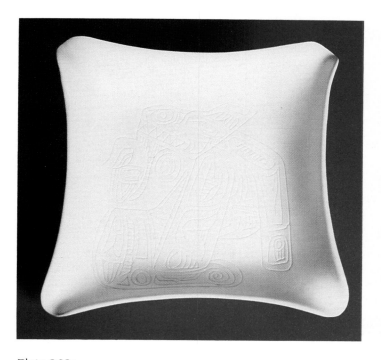

Plate 263:
7" square dish, sgraffito Mayan design on matte white, unsigned, $500.00, estate

Plate 264:
10" elliptical box, dark green stylized butterfly on cream ground, full signature on front, 1962, $650.00

Plate 265:
10" footed bowl, style C14, slightly carved abstract designs, full signature underside, $375.00 (rim chip)

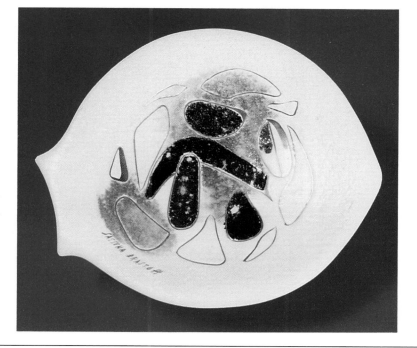

For De Wayne
Best Wishes!
Sascha Brastoff
7/10/90 ♥

Plate 266:
10" plate, white bamboo leaves on black ground, fine gold highlights, with underside inscription to author, priceless

Plate 267:
11½" pie plate, early piece, stylized "Amish" rooster, full signature on front, $600.00, estate (small chip)

Plate 268:
10" plate, classic Sascha rooster on white ground, full signature, $750.00
11" plate, classic Sascha rooster on gold ground, full signature, $400.00 (quake victim)
8" plate, slip decorated rooster on orange ground, full signature/1958, $550.00

Plate 269:
18" x 24" pastel, crucifix, full signature and dated; 1965, $1,100.00
(collection of Albert Guarino, Los Angeles)

Plate 270: MINIATURE GOLD-PLATED SCULPTURE (l to r)

5" sea nymph on Italian marble base, brass signature plate, $350.00

6" plumed horse on Italian marble base, brass signature plate, $750.00

5" seahorse in algae wreath, on Italian marble base, brass signature plate, $450.00

5" fish in Italian marble base, brass signature plate, $450.00

(far left, bottom)

...original rubber mold for sea nymph figure. Mold is made out of dental impression rubber.

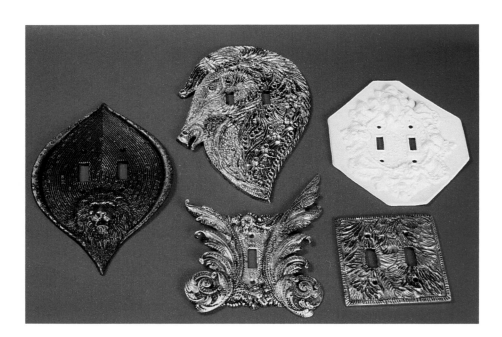

Plate 271: LIGHT SWITCHPLATES (clockwise from left)

9½" switchplate, lion's head, dull brass finish, "Sascha" in production mold, $100.00, estate

10" switchplate, horse's head, shiny brass finish, molded signature, $100.00, estate

6½" x 7½" switchplate, bisque fired ceramic prototype, molded signa-ture, $125.00, estate

4½" x 4½" switchplate, hand carved plastic prototype, no signature, paper label, $100.00, estate

9½" switchplate, hand carved plastic prototype, etched signature underside, $175.00, estate

Plate 272:
13½", style S12, Percheron horse, antique crackle glaze, obscured signature, $1,200.00, estate

Plate 273 (l to r): HORSES
11", "post factory," made by American Bisque Porcelains, Inc., with signature decal, $95.00
10½" prancing horse, style S1, pink with platinum overspray, 1 leg missing, commercial signature, $175.00
13", style MS10, mosaic pattern in rare solid yellow, unsigned, paper label, from Sascha's cactus garden, $300.00, estate

Plate 274:
11½" plate, sgraffito figure on matte black ground, titled "Dancer", from 1966 Dalzell Hatfield exhibit, in original frame, $1,400.00, estate

Plate 275:
10" plate, 3 angels on white ground, full signature, 1957, in original frame, $1,200.00, estate

Plate 276:
19" magnesium sculpture (including base), foo dog, gold plated, with etched brass signature plate, $1,800.00, estate

Plate 277:
14" metal sculpture, "Knight", gold plated, unsigned, $1,400.00, estate

Plate 278:
12½" magnesium sculpture (including base), owl with glass eyes, gold plated, signed, 1966, $1,000.00, estate

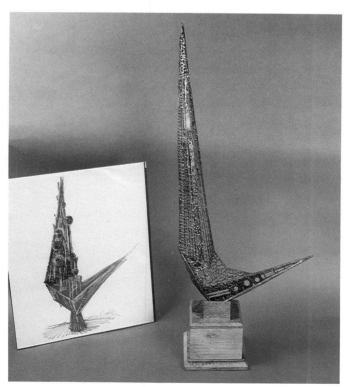

Plate 279:
24" welded metal sculpture, "The Quest", prototype for 14' version produced for Winthrop Rockefeller's Tower Building in Little Rock, Arkansas, 1960 (see Chapter 2), with description plate, shown with original drawing; $1,500.00, estate

Plate 280:
35" welded copper sculpture (including driftwood base), "Neptune's Daughter", gold plated, $3,750.00, estate

Plate 281: LAMPS
20" lamp base, style L248,
"Venetian" (abstract
design), commercial sig-
nature, $250.00
26" pair of lamps, style
L14A, "Tall Spool"
(abstract design), com-
mercial signature,
$900.00/pair*

*These lamps were actu-
ally made from a pair
of production candle-
sticks (top and bottom)
affixed to a cylindrical
vase in the center!

Plate 283:
12" charger, hand thrown, sgraffito image of two crowned skeletons embracing, full signature, 1962, $1,850.00, estate (collection of S.A. Conti)

Plate 282:
23" welded metal rod sculpture, "Pea Fowl", similar in design to that donated to the Los Angeles County Museum of Art in 1955, gold plated, $2,500.00, estate

Plate 284:
10" free form dish, sgraffito image of astral face on dark ground, full signature, 1958, $1,100.00

Plate 285:
7" three footed bowl,
stylized caricature of
Neptune, full signa-
ture, 1962, $975.00

Plate 286:
10" plate, matte blue with two
figures outlined in gold, full
signature, $1,000.00

Plate 287:
10" plate, "Americana," unsigned,
$800.00 estate

Plate 288:
12" plate, bull terrier "Nicky", early
commercial signature "Sascha B",
rare, $200.00

Plate 289:
8½" x 16" tiles (pair), style CP4, "Harlequin", with original metal hangers, commercial signature, $800.00 (pair)

Plate 290:
6½" x 8½" tiles (pair), native dancers, very early pieces in original frames, commercial signature, $900.00 (pair)

Plate 291:
12" x 12" tile, enamel on copper, miniature study for large mural commissioned by Winthrop Rockefeller for the lakeside boathouse of his Arkansas ranch, full signature, 1958, $1,250.00, estate

Plate 292:
16" x 20" tile, fruit bowl, slip decorated, commercial signature, $800.00

Plate 293:
21" x 9" tile, style CP3, "Temple Towers", in original custom frame, commercial signature, $375.00

Plate 294: PROMOTIONAL PIECES (clockwise from left)

12" "Jewel Bird" ashtray, style F6, personalized to R.M. Francis, commercial signature, $95.00

15" tray, style O52, designed for "Fiesta Pools", commercial signature, $175.00

10" free form dish, style F42, for "Fiesta Pools", commercial signature, $100.00

10" free form dish, style F42, for "Brown-Foreman", 1957, unsigned, $75.00

8" pitcher, no style #, "Brown-Foreman", commercial signature, $85.00

10" free form dish, style F3, created for "Cole of California", rare, commercial signature, $75.00 (center)

Plate 295: PROMOTIONAL PIECES (clockwise from left)

6" dish, no style number or factory decal, "Menasco Mfg. Co. 9/30/55", commercial signature, $75.00

12" ashtray, style O8, inscribed "In appreciation Richard M. Nixon from THE GUARDIANS of the Jewish Home for the Aged", circa 1968, commercial signature and registered trademark symbol, very rare, $150.00

8" dish, no style number, "Rooftops", person-alized for John Long, with Texaco flying horse as weathervane, commercial marks, $75.00

5" dish, style O3, element symbols, commercial marks, $65.00

5" dish, early piece, unmarked, sgraffito flower, personalized for actress Marjorie Reynolds, very rare, $100.00 (rim chip)

8" free form dish, "Revell, Inc.", all commercial marks, $75.00

Plate 296: AMERICANA (clockwise from left)
Dish, style O3B, 8", $65.00
Free form dish, style F42, 10", $45.00 (rim chip)
Free form dish, style F42, 10", $75.00
Free form dish, style F3, 10", $30.00 (rim chips)
Covered box, style O21, 7", $125.00
Bowl, style C5, 9", $70.00

Plate 297: AMERICANA
Ashtray, style O9, 17", $140.00 (rear) | Ashtrays, style O56A, 7", $45.00 (each) (front)

Plate 298: BALLET (clockwise from left)
Vase, 9", $175.00
Tortilla dish (covered), 9", $150.00 | (these are early pieces from the first factory)
Vase, 5", $75.00

Plate 299: PERSIAN (clockwise from top)
Platter, no style number, 14", $185.00
Free form dish, style F42, 10", $195.00
Ashtray, style F2, 8", $75.00
Dish, style F40, 10", $100.00

Ashtray, style O7, 10", $125.00
Covered box, style O23, 5", $225.00
 (center)

Plate 300: PERSIAN (clockwise from top)

Tea canister (missing top), no style number, 13", very rare, $250.00

Ashtray, style F2, 8", $75.00

Vase, style F21, 7", $95.00

Dish, style F40, 10", $95.00

Plate 301: PERSIAN

12" free form ashtray depicting Sascha's two pet Afghans, commercial signature but done by S.B. himself. (These two dogs were often seen romping on the rooftop of Sascha's West Los Angeles factory.) $575.00 (collection of S.A. Conti)

Plate 302: PAGODA (clockwise from left)
Bowl, style F26, 8", $135.00
Bowl, style F46, 11", $225.00
Vase, style O47, 8", $100.00

Dish, style C2, 7", $45.00
Dish, style O3, 5", $45.00
Dish, style C2, 7", $45.00

Plate 303: VANITY FAIR (clockwise from left)
Dish, style O3B, 8", $85.00
(with original factory label underside)
Three footed bowl, no style number, 10", $125.00

Ashtray, style O5, 7", $85.00
Ashtray, style F2, 8", $90.00
Dish, style O3, 5", $75.00
Nut dish, style O1, 3", $35.00

Plate 304: FOO DOG
16" long, matte black with gold, factory decal, $425.00

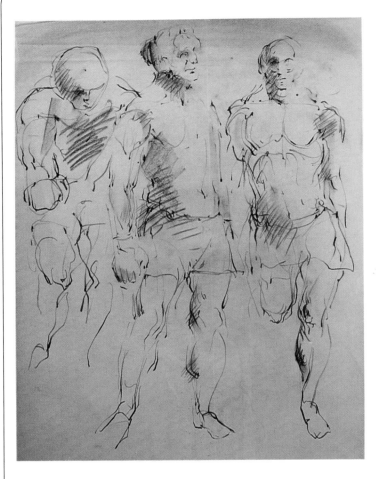

Plate 306:
12" x 16" charcoal and pastel of satyr,
unsigned, $350.00, estate

Plate 305:
18" x 24" charcoal of 3 runners, unsigned, $450.00,
estate

Plate 307:
18" x 19" charcoal and pastel, "Martian Love Affair",
unsigned, $425.00, estate

Plate 308:
18" x 24" charcoal and pastel of two caballeros, signed, 1965,
  $650.00
(collection of Hal Cunningham, Los Angeles, California)

Plate 309:
12" x 18" pastel of a lemur, signed, 1965, $600.00, estate

Plate 310:
18" x 24" charcoal and gold crayon of humanoid rooster, unsigned, $450.00, estate

Plate 311:
12" x 18" pastel of unidentified female, signed, 1965, $550.00, estate

Plate 312:
18" x 24" pastel of an organ grinder's monkey, signed, 1965, $850.00, estate

Plate 313:
18" x 24" pastel of nude woman with veil, signed, 1965, $850.00, estate

Plate 314:
18" x 24" pastel of mythical princess, signed, $750.00, estate

Plate 315:
12" x 18" pastel, "Catwoman", signed, 1965, $750.00, estate

Plate 316:
15" x 22½" charcoal and pastel, "Transformation", unsigned, $400.00, estate

Plate 317:
15" x 22" charcoal, "Staghorn Goddess", signed, $550.00, estate

Plate 318:
18" x 24" watercolor, "Fantasy In Fuchsia", signed,
1965, $700.00, estate

Plate 319:
18" x 24" charcoal and watercolor of
medieval boy holding candle,
signed, $600.00, estate

Plate 320:
15" x 23" charcoal of winged thurifer, unsigned, $400.00, (collection of Richard B. Flynn, Los Angeles, California)

Plate 321:
19½" x 22½" charcoal and pastel on newspaper of male with elaborate headdress, signed, 1965, very rare medium, $900.00, estate

Plate 322:
19½" x 22½" charcoal and pastel on newspaper, "The Three Faces Of Eve", signed, 1965, very rare medium, $900.00, estate

Plate 323:
18" x 24" pastel of provincial rooster, unsigned, $375.00, estate

Plate 324:
18" x 24" pastel and watercolor, "The Virgin Mary", signed, 1965,
$650.00, estate

Plate 325:
19" x 24" watercolor, costume design for Carmen Miranda, circa 1946,
   unsigned, rare $650.00, estate

Plate 326:
13" x 17" watercolor, costume design of plastic dress for Carmen Miranda used in film *If I'm Lucky*, circa 1946, unsigned, very rare, $600.00, estate

Plate 327:
11" x 15" pencil sketch and watercolor, personal dress design for Carmen Miranda (check out the platform shoes!), circa 1946, unsigned, very rare, $450.00, estate

Plate 328:
18" x 24" pencil sketch and watercolor, costume design for
Carmen Miranda, impressed seal "Sascha Brastoff 1947",
signed, with attached fabric swatches, extremely rare,
$950.00, estate. (collection of Bill Seay)

Plate 329:
18" x 24" watercolor, costume sketch for "Acapulco" scene in 1946 film *Diamond Horseshoe*,
unsigned, $300.00, estate

Plate 330:
15" x 20" charcoal and watercolor, costume sketch for "Acapulco" scene in 1946 film *Diamond Horseshoe*, unsigned,
$300.00, estate

Plate 331:
18" x 24" pastel costume sketch, signed, 1965, $750.00, estate (collection of Bill Seay)

Plate 332:
Assortment of hand sculpted styrofoam artware, flower pots and decorations known as "Hortisculpture", photographed in the grotto of Mr. Bethany's Los Angeles home. These pieces were never marketed and are most difficult to assign contemporary prices. Range $50.00 – $250.00 each depending upon condition and complexity of design.

Plate 333: JEWELRY (l to r in 4 rows)
Original jewelry tags

A. Christmas "snowflake" earrings, gold plated, $50.00/pair

B. Cuff links, hand painted on porcelain with gold plated backs, "Sascha B", very rare, $350.00/pair

C. Mask ring, sterling with ruby eyes (on original wooden stand), $500.00, estate

D. Silver pendant with child's head (shows traces of red wax from mold), $200.00, estate

E. Very ornate native mask pendant of jeweler's bronze, may also be mounted as decorative piece ("Living Jewelry"), $300.00, estate

F. 14K solid gold chain composed of 28 nude male figures, each is a separate movable link, marked "SB", $3,500.00*

G. Gold plated Sunburst pendant, rough surface, multi-produced piece marketed through the Merle Norman Co., $100.00

H. Heavy 14K gold pendant of mythical man with ram's horns and wings, diamond eyes, "scratched" initials "SB", $2,500.00*

I. Heavy 14K gold pendant of Mayan male, "scratched" initials "SB", $1,900.00*

J. Heavy 14K gold figure of Tibetan god holding a lightning bolt, "scratched" Sascha, $2,000.00*

K. Heavy 14k gold pendant of male and female, "scratched" initials "SB", $1,800.00*

L. Ornate owl mask of jeweler's bronze, may also be mounted as decorative piece ("Living Jewelry"), inscribed "Sascha", $300.00, estate

M. Gold plated Medusa pendant, multi-produced piece marketed through the Merle Norman Co., impressed "Sascha", $100.00

N. 14K yellow and white gold pendants of human hand, $300.00 each*

O. Gold plated dove pendant, "scratched" Sascha, $100.00*

P. Abstract design pendant of brass on jeweler's bronze, $150.00*

Q. Very ornate native mask pendant of jeweler's bronze, may also be mounted as decorative piece ("Living Jewelry"), impressed "Sascha", $300.00*

*all starred items were from Sascha's personal collection.

Plate 334: METAL SCULPTURE (clockwise from left)

"Starfish Elephant", gold plated, unsigned, $200.00, estate

"Ming Tree", gold plated, Italian marble base, original paper label, $350.00

"The Mask", bronze figure on rock base, original signature on brass plate, $1,900.00

"Mermaid", bronze figure with gold plated "coral reef", Italian marble base, brass signature plate, $500.00, estate

"Dancing Harvest Child" figures (2), 6", gold plated bronze, $500.00 each (collection of Bill Seay)

"Caught in a Web", gold plated female figure embedded in lucite (paperweight), $350.00, estate

Plate 335: MORE GOLD! (clockwise from left)
Covered urn, style O95, 7", $150.00
Bowl, style O93, 10", $130.00
Vase, style 181 R, 8", $95.00
Vase with enamel top, no style number,
12", rare, $250.00
Dish, style F3 R, 10", $35.00
Dish, style O3, 5", $55.00

Plate 336: MOSAIC (clockwise from top left)

Dish, style M7, 12", $90.00 (high gloss)
Vase, style M73, 8", $140.00

Dish, style M7, 12", $100.00 (matte)
Dish, style M20, 5", $30.00 (each)
Dish, style M5, 8", $80.00

Plate 337:
13" x 15" solid bronze Percheron horse, 1 of 4 ever produced; 1 of 2 owned by Mr. Bethany, $4,500.00, estate

A PARTIAL SHOWING OF ORIGINALS FROM THE COLLECTION OF BILL SEAY

Plate 338:
11" x 12" plastic prototype, "Equus", metallic coating, mounted on petrified wood base, signed, 1970, $850.00, estate

Plate 339:
10" plate, "Fall of the House of Usher", full signature on front, $850.00

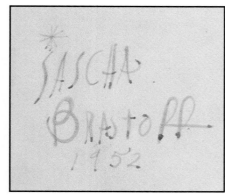

Plate 340:
10" plate, abstract design — gold, charcoal and white, full signature, 1952, as shown, $650.00

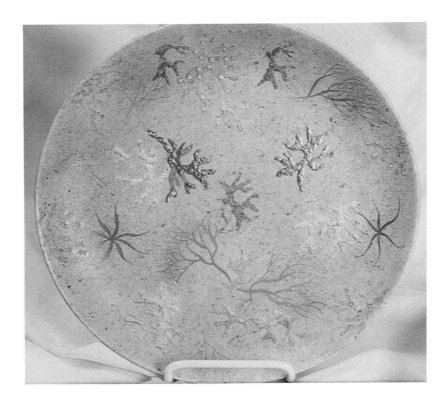

Plate 341:
10" plate depicting marine
life, full signature, $750.00

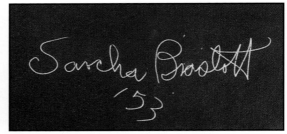

Plate 342:
11½" plate, "Daliesque" male figure on black
matte finish, fully signed on front and back,
an exceptionally fine example of Sascha's
early 1950s modern work, $1,350.00

Plate 343:
10" plate depicting 3 native dancers, signed, factory acquisition, $875.00

Plate 344:
11½" hand thrown plate, leaves on blue ground, unfired experimental, etched full signature on back, factory acquisition, $400.00

Plate 345:
11" plate, stylized provincial rooster on heavy gold ground, unsigned, factory acquisition, $550.00

Plate 346:
10" plate of rooster, full signature on front, $700.00

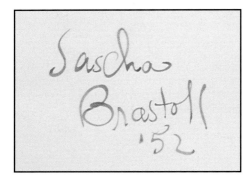

Plate 347:
10" plate depicting bizarre, abstract rooster, fully signed on front and back (shown), $750.00

Plate 348:
11½" plate, slip decorated turnips, full signature, $650.00

Plate 349:
8" square ashtray of fish detailed with very fine gold work, full signature, 1953, $600.00

Plate 350:
10" ashtray, sgraffito image of "Star Steed" on black matte finish, full signature, $1,200.00

Plate 351: 6" x 6" TILES (l to r)
Rooster tiles, set of 3, signed "Sascha B", $125.00 each (rear)
"Isadora Duncan" line drawing, unsigned, factory chip on corner, $50.00

Rooster, fully signed, $250.00
"Butterfly Girl", fully signed, $300.00
(all of the above were factory acquisitions)

Plate 352: 6" x 6" TILES
"Rooftops", set of 3 created as fabric design, unsigned, $150.00/set (rear)
"Americana" people, created for fabric design, unsigned, $100.00/pair (front)
(all of the above were factory acquisitions)

Plate 353:
6" x 6" tile depicting demon outlined in heavy gold on cobalt ground, full signature, $300.00

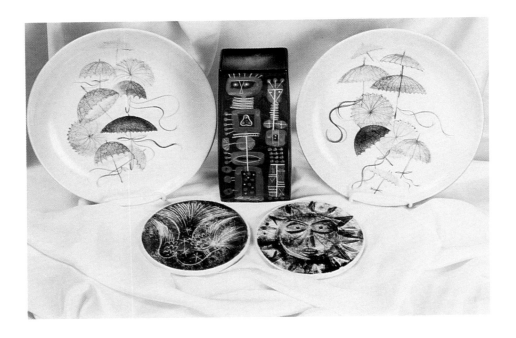

Plate 354:

10" plates (pair), "The Umbrellas of Cherbourg", fully signed (as shown below), $1,250.00/pair (rear)

10" vase, early piece showing space creatures, 2 full signatures, $900.00 (rear)

6" round tile of Picasso-like sunburst, fully signed, $300.00 (front)

6" round tile of Jewel Bird, signed "Sascha B", $200.00 (front)

(all were factory acquisitions)

Plate 355:
10" plate depicting ultra-stylized telephone repairmen, very 1950s!,
full signature, $1,000.00

Plate 356: THREE ORIGINAL 8" PORCELAIN PLATES (l to r)

Sgraffito image of goddess, very intricate gold application, fully signed, $700.00
Daliesque "Lizard Baying at the Moon", fully signed, NPA

Native figure on celadon green ground, fully signed, restored, $175.00

Plate 357:
11" china plate, experimental children's pattern (never produced), unsigned, factory acquisition, $250.00

Plate 358: THREE ORIGINAL PLATES (l to r)

10", "Desdemona" in fine gold outline on faux raku ground, signed "Sascha", factory acquisition, $950.00

10", 2 blue fish, heavily detailed in blue and gold, full signature, 1953, kiln flaw, $550.00

9" porcelain, tribute to Jean Cocteau, unsigned, from factory, $350.00

Plate 359: THREE ORIGINAL 10" PLATES (l to r)

Abstract bullseye, fully signed on back, 1952, $600.00

"Stained glass" rooster, fully signed, $650.00

Pony on black matte finish, personalized to Bill Seay, fully signed, NFS

Plate 360:
11½" plate, bowl of arranged flowers, full signature, $900.00

Plate 361:
14" charger, gray and white face-less nude female, full signature, original frame, $1,100.00, estate

Plate 362:
Three 10" plates of mythical women created as a
   series, fully signed and in original frame,
   $1,850.00, estate

THE BETHANY COLLECTION (CONT.)

Plate 363: STAR STEED (clockwise from left)
3 footed bowl, no style number, 9", $85.00
Ashtray, style F8, 17", $150.00
Vase, style O47, 8", $75.00

Free form dish, style C3, 7", $40.00 (center)
Covered boxes, no style number (early), 5", $35.00 – $45.00 each

Plate 364: STAR STEED (clockwise from left)
Ashtray, style O6, 8", $55.00
Square Tray, style O52, 15", $225.00
Ashtray, no style number (early), 9", $55.00

Ashtray, no style number (early), 6", $35.00 – $45.00
Vase, style F21, 7", $75.00 (center)

Plate 365: STAR STEED (clockwise from left)
Ashtray, style O5, 7", $40.00
Cachepot, no style number (early), 5", $75.00 (rim flake)
Footed bowl, style C14, 10", $75.00

Covered box, no style number (early), 5", $35.00 – $45.00
Ashtray, style O8A, 8", $30.00

Plate 366:
23½" "Tree of Life" 5 light candlestick, very early experimental piece in smoke tree design, one-of-a-kind, restored, $2,200.00 (collection of Bill Seay)

Plate 367: ROMAN COIN FINE CHINA
(In rare and unusual cocoa brown)
Five piece place setting, $250.00
Coffee pot, $200.00

Sugar/creamer, $250.00
Ceramic advertising sign, NFS

Plate 368: "EARLY" TANKARDS
Set of 6 tankards, 5", each
depicting different type of
fruit, $300.00/set
Ceramic advertising sign, NFS

Plate 369: RESIN (clockwise from left)
Votive candle holder, 10", raised grapes, green, etched "Sascha B" and ®, $35.00 each
Votive candle holder, 9", vertical carving, red, etched "Sascha B" and ®, $35.00
Candle holder, 10", native faces (both sides), green, etched "Sascha B" and ®, from previous ceramic design of Sascha's, $75.00
Votive candle holder, 6", vertical carving, blue, etched "Sascha B" and ®, $25.00
Octopus, 9½" tall, orange, etched "Sascha B" and ®, $350.00
Hippo, 10" long, blue, etched "Sascha B" and ®, $350.00

According to Filomena Bruno, these pieces were acquired or bought at retail trade shows after Sascha left his West Los Angeles factory in the early 1960s. As we discussed in Chapter 3, the company retained the right to use Sascha's name on either newly produced items or those purchased. The company simply reissued previously produced designs or added his name to acquired ones. These resin pieces were signed "Sascha B" and an additional ® was added. In reality, Sascha had absolutely nothing to do with the design or creation of these pieces. Steve Conti spoke to avid resin animal collector Michael DiMaria who has a piece with an original paper label stating, "designed exclusively for Sascha Brastoff by Richard Wenger." They are very highly prized by collectors today, and, as listed, the animals are quite expensive. We feel they are very much like something Sascha would have designed — whimsical, colorful, and animated. Other animals, such as the polar bear or octopus, were also made in brightly colored resin. Some of these pieces bear the copyright symbol instead of the registered trademark. See Chapter 4 for more details.

Plate 370: POODLE (clockwise from top left)
All of these poodle pieces are marked "Sascha B" & ® as explained above and in Chapter 4. Sascha did create and produce his own line of custom painted and inscribed poodle, dog, and cat plates as early as 1948. However, these examples are post factory.

Ashtray, style H6, 7", $75.00
Free form dish, style F40, 10", $75.00
Ashtray, style O14, 9", $75.00
Ashtray, style H1, 5", $65.00
Ashtray, style O12, 7", $60.00
Ashtray, style H3, 6", $65.00
Ashtray, style H6, 7", $75.00 (center)
("H" series indicate "hooded")

Plate 371: PROVINCIAL ROOSTER (l to r)
Vase, style F20, 5", experimental combination of rooster image on faux raku background, complete with glazing instructions (by Sascha) written on bottom, $350.00, estate
Ashtray, style F6A, 10", $90.00
Rubber mold created with lost wax process for jewelry production, $100.00, estate

Plate 372: EXPERIMENTAL PORCELAIN DINNER PLATES
7 pieces from Sascha's own kitchen — all originals and all unmarked & unsigned. Sascha would buy blank white dinner plates (10" – 12"; from other manufacturers) and create designs on them. These were part of 17 pieces purchased from the estate. Valued at $100.00 each.

Plate 373: EXPERIMENTAL CERAMIC PLATES
6 pieces also from Sascha's home; unmarked and unsigned. Valued at
$100.00 each.

Plate 374: (l to r)
10" experimental ceramic plate, heavy gold work and sgraffito designs, UNSIGNED, $100.00, estate

11" porcelain plate, abstract sunburst in gold, full signature on back, 1957, $450.00 (Bill Seay's)

Plate 375: CHI CHI BIRDS (clockwise from left)

Covered box, style O23, 5", $200.00 (factory acquisition of Bill Seay)
Vase, style F20, 5", $85.00
Tray, style O52, 15", $100.00 (rim chip)
Plate, no style number, 11", $65.00 (kiln flaws)

Ashtray, style F6, 12", $90.00
Dish, style O3, 5", $60.00
Ashtray, style O7, 10", $80.00
Covered box, no style number, 11", $100.00 (center)

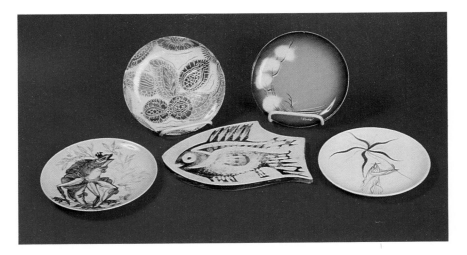

Plate 376: (clockwise from top left)

6" plate, sgrafitto leaf design, full signature, 1959, $400.00 (Bethany's)

7" plate, early "Smoke Tree" in rare rust color, $30.00 (collection of A. Guarino)

7" plate, female figure in gold on white, signed Sascha B but personally done by Sascha $250.00 (Seay's)

9" fish trivet, decorated by Sascha and acquired by Seay while at the factory, unsigned, $150.00

7" plate depicting minute detail of frog prince, fully signed on front & back, NPA (Seay's)

...WE CONTINUE THE BETHANY COLLECTION

Plate 377: ASSORTED METALWORK (clockwise from top left)

Plaque, "Star Steed", enamel on copper, 12", $550.00, estate

Tray, "Capricorn Horse", hand etched copper, 12", $750.00, estate

Plaque, "Star Steed", brass limited edition, 1978, 12", $250.00 (Conti's)

Plaque, "Wide Eyed Cat", white metal, 5" x 7", $175.00

Plaque, "Pheasant", white metal, 8" x 9", $200.00

Plaque, "Star Steed" advertising piece, brass, 3" x 6", $150.00

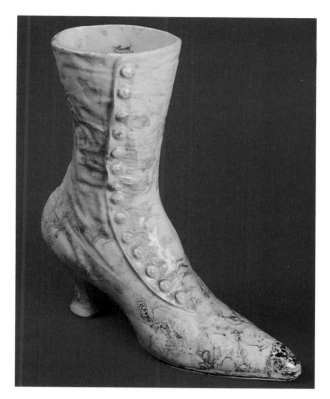

Plate 378:
Victorian high button shoe in ceramic
with Surf Ballet glaze, 10", $200.00

Plate 379: ROOSTERS (l to r)
Matte white "pebble" finish, 17", restored by Bill Seay, $150.00
repaired comb, $195.00
Real gold leaf, 17", full signature,
Platinum and powder blue, 23", $425.00, estate
damaged in the L.A. quake and

Plate 380:
Very early terra cotta prancing horse (circa 1940), as found in Sascha's home studio. The earliest example of his handmade "New York Clay Club" type work we've found, 9" with wood base, NPA.

Plate 381: HOLOGRAPHIC JEWELRY (l to r)
(Look closely for image!)
"King Neptune" oval pendant with gold plated bezel and chain, signed "Sascha", $100.00
"Owl" bolo with original leather strap. This was Sascha's favorite personal hologram and was worn on many occasions, signed, $150.00

"Sunburst" small pendant, gold plated bezel, $75.00
"Mask of King Tut" in gold plated beaded bezel, $100.00
"Gemini" in gold plated bezel, $100.00

(All of our holograms were from Sascha's estate)

Plate 382: UNFRAMED HOLOGRAMS
A selection of 15 different unframed holograms from Sascha's home studio. It is extremely difficult to photograph a hologram as light intensity and direction are crucial to showing each individual image. Look closely and see how fabulous they are! Valued at $100.00 each, estate.

Plate 383: CHRISTMAS ORNAMENTS
A selection of 12 punched metal (probably brass and white metal) Christmas ornaments produced in a limited edition, circa 1978. These items were from the estate and have never before been seen in stores. Two of the group are in their original packaging. Valued at $75.00 each.

FROM THE SEAY COLLECTION

Plate 384: (with reverse shot)
20" figure of native man, special finish commissioned by Sascha from Seay's father, truly one of a kind, $2,000.00

Plate 385: (with reverse shot)
13" candlestick vase, early piece (from first factory), with original paper label, rare, $850.00

Plate 386:
10½" lamp, made from ceramic tea canister (unwired), full signature, $800.00

Plate 388:
10" plate, owl on dark ground, full signature, $500.00

Plate 387
Bowl depicting fish, full signature, $550.00 | Ashtray, marine motif, full signature, $500.00

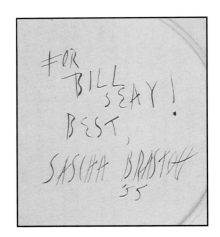

Plate 389:
11" plate, porcelain dinnerware of Provincial Rooster, fully signed, inscribed, and dated, $600.00

Plate 390:
11" plate, hand thrown and unfired of 3 leaves, with full signature over kiln instructions, NPA

Plate 391:
11" plate depicting ghost-like figures, $650.00, estate

Plate 392:
10" free form dish of court jester, full signature, one of the finest examples we've seen, $900.00

Plate 393:
11" plates depicting male and female dancers, full signatures underside, $950.00/pair

Plates 394:
11" plate, specially produced by Sascha for Howard Shoup as Christmas gift, with signature, NPA

Plate 395:
11" plate depicting intricately detailed dragon, a very fine example of Sascha's work, $950.00

THE BETHANY COLLECTION

Plate 396:
18" x 24" charcoal of Sascha's pet
   monkey Liz, full signature, 1965,
   $750.00, estate

Plate 397:
18" x 24" pastel, "Dumbo", unsigned,
   $250.00, estate

Plate 398:
16" x 22" pastel, hippo, unsigned,
   $350.00, estate

Plate 399:
12" x 18" pastel & black crayon of Picasso-like draped female, full signature, 1965, $500.00, estate

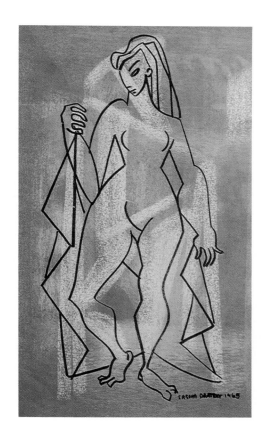

Plate 400:
8" x 10" pastel of Juliet, full signature, 1965, $450.00, estate

Plate 401:
12" x 16" pastel of floral bouquet, full signature, 1965, $450.00, estate

Plate 402:
18" x 24" pastel of floral rooster, full signature, 1965, $500.00, estate

Plate 403:
9½" x 15" pastel & crayon of female in maid's outfit, partially signed (torn corner), very early and rare piece, $600.00, estate

ASSORTED SCRATCHBOARD DRAWINGS
Plates 404–409 (all are estate items)

Plate 404:
11" x 14" sunburst, signed, $750.00

Plate 405:
11" x 14", "Floral Lady", signed, $750.00

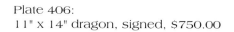

Plate 406:
11" x 14" dragon, signed, $750.00

Plate 407:
11" round "Star Steed", signed, $650.00

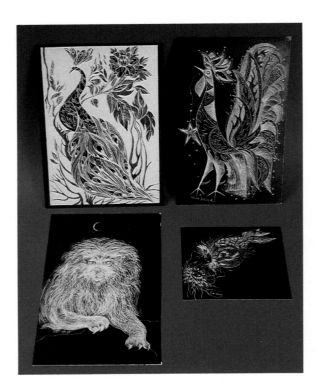

Plate 409: (l to r)
11" x 14" scratch-board of cockatiel, signed, $750.00
11½" statue from   American Bisque Porcelains, Inc. (factory mark), $125.00

Plate 408: (clockwise from top left)
7" x 10¼" peacock, signed, $550.00
7" x 11" rooster, signed, $600.00
"She-fish", $450.00
Lion, $500.00

EARLY PIECES (from first factory (quonset hut) and/or "Tom Hamilton's"

Plate 410:
12" lamp bases, flowers on green ground, "Sascha B", $350.00/pair

Plate 411:
12" x 19" platter, sgraffito fish, "Sascha B", $350.00 (collection of Jerry McKenna, Los Angeles, California)

Plate 412: (all signed "Sascha B")
8" dishes, $60.00–$75.00 each; 4 shown | 10" vase, large and rare, $300.00

Plate 413:
8" dish depicting masted ship, probably done as custom order, "Sascha B", rare, $100.00

Plate 414: (all signed "Sascha B")
12½" vase, $225.00
9" ashtray, $75.00
8" peach/watermelon plates, $50.00–$60.00
    each

5" dish, gray w/strawberries and pear,
    (center), $40.00–$50.00

Plate 415: (clockwise from top left; all signed "Sascha B")

14" chop plate, $120.00–$135.00 (Sascha loved this dark shade of green and used it on many of his early ceramics. This simple leaf pattern was used to test out new artists applying for staff positions at all of Sascha's factories!)

10" sectional dish, $85.00
8" fish, $75.00–$95.00
7" lidded box, $75.00–$85.00
7" pitcher, $85.00 (collection of Bill Seay)
11" vase, (center), $140.00–$175.00

Plate 416: (all signed "Sascha B")
12" plate, strawberry, $75.00–$95.00
12" plate, farmyard, $85.00–$100.00

7" x 9" tile, $100.00

Plate 417: EARLY TILES (l to r; all signed "Sascha B")
7" x 9", $100.00
7" x 9", $125.00 rare color & texture

7" x 9", $100.00

Plate 418: SMOKE TREE IN CERAMIC (clockwise from top left)

14" platter, slightly worn gold, $35.00–$50.00

7" plate, rare rust color, $30.00 (collection of Al Guarino, Los Angeles, California)

5" three-footed bowl, $40.00–$50.00

9" bowl, $25.00–$35.00

Coffee cups, $15.00/each

Plate 419: SMOKE TREE

10" ceramic plate, experimental piece done by Sascha and signed, $300.00 estate

9" porcelain plate, full signature on back, 1959, $350.00

Plate 420: ASSORTED POTS/SUGARS (clockwise from left)

8" tall, leaf design, rooster mark, $125.00

7" porcelain depicting Parisian scene, $95.00 (lid not shown)

10" tall, gray, rooster mark, $125.00

7" Vanity Fair leaf pattern, early, $35.00–$45.00

4" Roman Coin, porcelain, gray, $125.00 (lid not shown)

Plate 421:
13" fruit bowl, large and impressive early piece, $175.00–$200.00

Plate 422: AFRICAN MASKS
10", style K11 (female), commercially produced but hard to find, $350.00
10", style K11 (female), hand painted and fully signed by Sascha, $1,200.00 estate
ceramic display sign NPA, estate

Plate 423:
9" porcelain plate by French artist
Marcel Vertés, made during his
1957 visit to factory as told in
Chapter 2, underside signature,
$550.00

Plate 424:
13" x 14" ceramic horse (with 2
  saddle bags), antique crackle
  glaze, inscribed to Bill Seay,
  signed and dated (1958),
  $1,750.00

Plate 425:
8" x 12" oil painting, "Masquerade", full signature, 1965,
$950.00 estate

Plate 426: CITRUS (l to r)
Free form dish, style F42, 10",
    $45.00–$60.00 (2 shown)

Ashtray, style O8, 12",
    $35.00–$45.00 (2 shown)

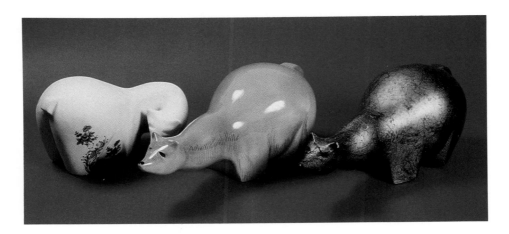

Plate 427: POLAR BEARS (l to r)
9", produced by American Bisque
    Porcelains, $95.00 estate
10", "post factory" piece signed

Sascha B and ®, $125.00, estate
10", rare gilt version, unsigned,
    $125.00–$145.00, estate

Plate 428:
MOSAIC CAT, Style MS11, 10", $85.00 (version was also produced by American Bisque Porcelains; $45.00)

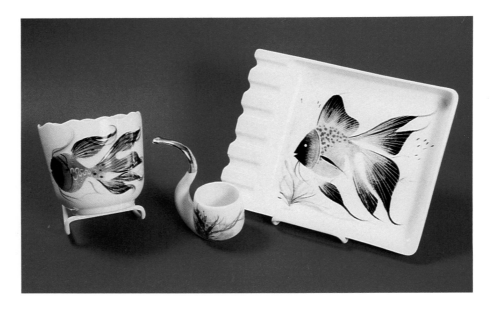

Plate 429: "EARLY FISH" (l to r)
4" cachepot, $85.00
4" pipe, $45.00

9" ashtray, $95.00

Plate 430: THE FRANKLIN MINT'S SILVER CIRCUS (see Chapter 3 for details)
A limited edition set of 6 figures produced in solid sterling silver with 24 karat gold accents,
$2,000/set estate. (Also shown: original sketches and wax model of lion)

Plate 431: A MULTI-COLOR ASSORTMENT OF "SURF BALLET" CERAMIC DINNERWARE
Sascha created the design for this "dipped" dinnerware back in the late 1940s and continued to produce it until the late 1950s. The line came in many colors: creamy white, pink, yellow, coral, dark green, light blue, cocoa brown, and black swirled with real gold or platinum. Because it was produced in such volume and over a long period of time, we find examples everywhere we shop. Prices are determined, of course, based on size, color, and condition of piece with large pieces and unusually small pieces being less common and more desirable.

Cup and saucer, $20.00–$40.00
10" plate, $15.00–$30.00
5" tankard, $20.00–$25.00

Sugar and creamer, $30.00–$40.00
Serving pieces, $40.00–$50.00

Plate 432:
Set of blue candle holders with raised platinum overglaze, $75.00

A pink sea shell with raised platinum overglaze, $65.00

Plate 433: SURF BALLET
A selection of black and brown dinnerware with gold.

Plate 434: SURF BALLET
An unusual and rare set of chalices from Sascha's
    estate (probably experimental) $350.00/set

Plate 435: AZTEC OR MAYAN DESIGNS (clockwise from top left)

All of these pieces are marked "Sascha B" & ®. Sascha was very much influenced by the Aztec and Mayan cultures after visiting their homelands. He created these designs before leaving his factory in 1962 although these pieces (with the registered trademark symbol) were produced after S.B. left his company.

Ashtray, style F40, 10", $60.00–$65.00
Chop plate, style O53, 17", $175.00
Candle holder, style S39, 10", $125.00 (this design was later made "post factory" in resin)
Ashtray, style H8, $85.00
Lighter, style L6, 6", $35.00–$40.00
Cigarette, style L1, 3", $20.00–$25.00

Plate 436: (clockwise from top left) *as marked in plate 435.

Dish, style O12, $65.00
Dish, style F8, 17", $125.00
3-footed dish, no style number, $50.00–$65.00

Ashtray, style H3 (w/original tag), $75.00
Dish, style C2, 7", $45.00

Plate 437: HAEGER POTTERY "ESPLANADE" (clockwise from left; consult Chapter 3 for more details) and see original catalog on page 110.

Octagonal lidded box, 5½", $50.00–$65.00
Rectangular lidded box, 8½", $45.00–$50.00
Jardiniere, $35.00

Rectangular lidded box, 8½", $45.00–$50.00
Ashtray, 6", $35.00–$40.00

Plate 438: ORANGE AND GOLD (clockwise from left; all marked "Sascha B" and ®)
Dish, style J10, $65.00
Plate, style T21, 11", $95.00
Covered bowl, style O35, $125.00–$145.00
Lidded box, style O22, $80.00–$95.00

Dish, style O3, 5", $30.00–$35.00 (2 shown)
Lighter set, style L34, $40.00–$60.00/set

Plate 439: MERBABY
24" x 27" pastel, prototype of plate design, signed, $550.00 estate

Plate 440: MERBABY (clockwise from top)

Chop plate, style O53, 17", $150.00
Pipe, style O82, 10", $65.00–$75.00
Plate, 9", $45.00–$60.00

Plate, 9", experiment in gold w/several signature variations on underside, $100.00 estate

Plate 441: ALASKA BY MATT ADAMS (clockwise from left; see Chapter 4 for details)
Bowl, 10", $35.00–$45.00
Bowl, style 190, 10", $50.00–$65.00
Pitcher, style 181A, $30.00–$45.00

Plates, 8", $25.00–$40.00/each (2 shown)
Shaker, 3", $20.00–$25.00 (center)

Plate 442: ALASKA BY BRASTOFF (clockwise from top left)

Dish, style C3, 7", "Sascha B" & ®, with original souvenir decal, $90.00

Egg, style O44A, 7", factory mark & signature, $75.00–$85.00 (lid not shown)

Dish, style J10, marked "Sascha B" & ®, $35.00–$45.00

Mug, style O77, marked "Sascha B" & ®, $25.00–$35.00

Sugar bowl, no style number, factory mark & signature, $65.00–$75.00

Ashtray, style H1, marked "Sascha B" & ®, $45.00–$60.00

Plate 443: ASSORTED NATIVE-THEMED PIECES BY BRASTOFF (clockwise from left)

Plate, 8", signed "Sascha B" (probably post 1953 "Alaska" piece), $85.00

Plate, 12", crayon-like depiction of Eskimo, an original signed "Sascha B", $550.00 estate

Tankard, early, signed "Sascha B", $65.00

Dish, early, no mark or signature, $30.00

Custard cup, no mark, signed "Sascha B", $40.00

Plate 444: "COPYKATS" — DESIGNS INFLUENCED BY BRASTOFF (clockwise from left; see Chapter 4)

9" ashtray (circa late 1950s) by Enesco Imports, Japan. This piece was an attempt to copy Sascha's Pagoda pattern, $12.00–$15.00 (collection of S.A. Conti)

9" vase signed "Sarena"; purportedly one of Kourishima's V.C.S. artists, $25.00

10" ceramic plate produced by the Homer Laughlin Co. in 1953. This "California Provincial" design is a direct knock-off of Sascha's provincial roosters, $20.00 (collection of S.A. Conti)

9" bowl (circa 1963) from Eddie Kourishima's Venice Clay Shops, Venice, CA, $30.00–$40.00

8" pipe (circa 1955) unmarked but probably Santa Anita Ware's version of Sascha's Surf Ballet glaze, $25.00

Plate 445:

14" ashtray, by Brastoff protegé Marc Bellaire, was reminiscent of S.B.'s Chi Chi Bird design. Titled "Bird Isle" (#B41-14), this is a finely decorated example of 1950s design, $140.00 (collection of Bill Seay)

Plate 446:
Sensational Marc Bellaire "Mardi Gras" lamp with red fiberglass shade, $375.00-425.00 (collection of Steve Conti)

Plate 447:
16" magnesium sculpture titled "Visitation" shown at the 1966 Dalzell Hatfield Gallery show. This metal creation is mounted on a redwood "fungal growth." Base bears the original brass signature plate. $3,600.00 (collection of Mr. Bethany and from Sascha's estate)

Plate 448:
9" x 12" watercolor done by Sascha in wartime Paris; 1945, extremely rare, $900.00 (col-
lection of Bill Seay)

Plate 449: ASSORTED FABRICS
Sascha's fabrics are extremely difficult to find in any quantity. We feel, due to their scarcity, they should sell for approximately $100.00–$300.00/yard, based upon the amount available, color, condition, etc. Good luck finding some of it! All of our examples are from Sascha's estate.

Plate 450: ASSORTED GILT TILES (clockwise from top left)
6" x 8½", "Floral Bouquet", $75.00
14" square, "Octopus", $100.00
11" diameter, "Capricorn Seagoat", $300.00
4" square tiles, 1 horse; 1 fish; both hand
signed, $35.00/each
6" x 8½" of bull, $75.00
8" diameter of sunburst, $60.00 (center)

Plate 451:
12" x 12" gold plated inset, created by Sascha, for one of the two
church podiums at St. Augustine-by-the-Sea. This piece was
not used in the church (reason
unknown) and is now part of Bill
Seay's collection, NPA

Plate 452: (l to r)
This handmade and gold plated
crucifix, circa 1972, is from the Al
Guarino collection, Los Angeles,
$375.00

This crucifix, first shown in 1966 at
the Dalzell Hatfield Gallery, is in
the collection of Arthur Green,
Los Angeles, NPA

Plate 453:
An assortment of waxes created by Sascha for either jewelry or sculpture (lost wax process) shown for your enjoyment, NPA.

Plate 454:
A handmade ceramic display figure used in 1969 at Esplanade (see Chapter 3). In addition to sculpting the extraordinary facial details and body, Sascha created the hair style out of human hair and made her garment, too! We salvaged 3 of these figures from the estate and each of us got to keep one. This one belongs to Mr. Bethany and is 16" tall, $2,500.00.

Plate 455: MOSAIC LAMPS (l to r)
"Serpent God", style LM-11, 38", with original matchstick shade, $550.00 "Fish", style M39, 27", $400.00

Plate 456:
Lamp, ovaloid, or egg-shaped, style L6A, 27", "Vanity Fair" design, with original shade, small base chip, $375.00

Plate 457: OBELISKS
Ceramic obelisk, no style number, 21" w/top (one top not shown), $750.00/each, estate

The "Vanity Fair" pattern obelisk (on left) was used in the 1956 film *Forbidden Planet.*

Plate 458:
18" x 24" charcoal of a contemporary female, fully signed and dated (1965), courtesy of Kozell and Sally Cannon Boren, $900.00

Plate 459:
14" candlestick centerpiece of family, circa 1949; a rare and hard to find example of Sascha's early work, from the collection of Diane Eberly, $1,000.00

Plate 460:
8" bottle of "Roly Poly" figure, a rare and early piece, collection of Diane Eberly, $850.00

Plate 461:
12" ceramic plate depicting mythical aquatic female, fully signed and dated on front, truly spectacular! This piece was also made available courtesy of Diane Eberly, $900.00

Plate 462:
Faun Mask, style M31, 13", collection of Diane Eberly, $750.00. (As seen on our book cover.)

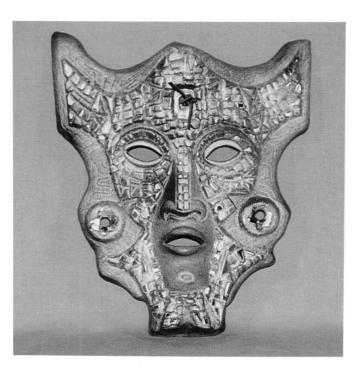

The following are from the collection of Daniel E. Fast, M.D. Los Angeles, California.

Plate 463:
Centerpiece, early "quonset hut," 10"x16½", full signature on front bottom
 right, $1,200.00

Plate 464:
11" porcelain plate, experimental
 design for dinnerware, decorated with Sascha's own finger-
 prints! A most unique and
 fabulous example of his creativity, signed (as shown), $600.00

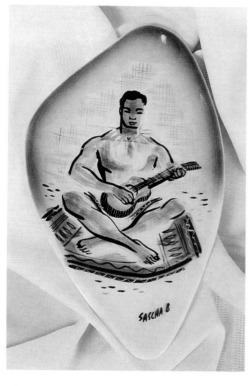

Plate 465:
Elephant, style S8, 7", originally sold as pair with opposing mate, heavy gold over pink, $300.00

Plate 466:
Dish, style F3, 10" depiction of Hawaiian boy playing guitar, $85.00

Plate 467:
Prancing horses, a very early example of Sascha's work, 10", "Sascha B" etched into bases, exceptional! $1,000.00/pair

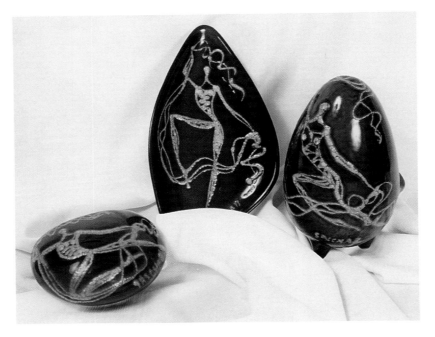

Plate 468: MINOS (l to r)
Ashtray, style H11, 6", $90.00
Dish, style F3, 10", $80.00
Bowl, style H7, 10", $125.00

(These pieces were produced in unusual tangerine over dark cocoa brown)

Plate 469: 7" Plate, very early sgraffito homage to Sascha's friend, costumer Howard Shoup, "Sascha B" on front, $350.00

Plate 470:
9" porcelain plate, experimental
piece with very fine gold work,
full signature (as shown), $650.00

Plate 471:
11" porcelain plates, both experimental and fully signed on back, $750.00
each.

Plate 472:
Dish, style 06, 8" depiction of Los Angeles City Hall and
personalized for Sam Lender, full signature on lower
left front, $600.00

Plate 473: ALASKA
Vase, style 094, 12", fully
signed on bottom, $575.00

Plate 474:
13" candlestick vase, early
piece (circa 1949), "Sascha
B" on side, $850.00

Plate 475: ROOFTOPS
Wall pocket, style 031, 20", $375.00

Plate 476:
Tile, "charcoal" portrait in original factory frame, 11" x 13", $900.00

Bronze advertising plaque, "Sascha Brastoff", entirely handmade, NFS

There's No Place Like Home

Shortly after Sascha's passing in 1993, the authors commissioned Los Angeles documentary film maker Rick Flynn to preserve the look of Sascha's modest home on film. These photos are the only known record of the West Los Angeles dwelling "as Sascha had left it."

Plate 477:
Astrology-themed Sascha plate.

Plate 478:
Wall in Sascha's den: 3-plates on right now belong to Bill Seay.

Plate 479:
North wall in Sascha's den; African mask on left is Mr. Bethany's.

Plate 481:
Wooden prototype for ceramic Foo Dog.

Plate 480:
Large fish tile circa 1951.

Plate 482:
Framed owl (collection of Bill Seay).

Plate 483:
"Premonition", collection of Min Wan, Seoul, Korea.

Plate 484
A lovely dove plate.

Plate 485:
A Sascha original from 1960.

Plate 486:
"Piranha" oil and gesso, fully signed and dated 1966; collection of
author S. A. Conti (also on cover).

Plate 487:
An abstract oil circa 1965.

Plate 488:
A large horizontal tile from S.B.'s living room.

Plate 489:
Sascha's backyard studio. Assorted magnesium sculpture.

Plate 490:
Sascha's studio.

Plate 491:
Studio.

Plate 492:
Prototype for Eastern – Indian themed chess set by Sascha; in front entryway.

Plate 493:
Assorted gold plated metal sculpture and Michael Landon's "Holocaust Star" lower right.

Plate 494:
The entryway.

Plate 495:
Sascha's living room, 1993.

Plate 496:
Bronze percheron horse (owned by Bethany) is on Eastlake Victorian parlor table.

Plate 497:
Victorian vanity served as a sideboard in Sascha's dining room. Skeleton plate (lower left) belongs to Steve Conti, "Faith Eternal" gold plated sculpture part of the Daniel E. Fast collection. Also, reflection of St. Augustine prototype cross owned by Bethany.

Plate 498:
Collection of Kozell and Sally Cannon Boren.

Plate 499:
Steel sculpture in garden.

Plate 500:
Another garden wall.

Plate 501:
Sascha's patio dining area.

Plate 502:
Shower tiles in backyard studio.

Plate 503:
Another wall in Sascha's dining room. Center enamel tile of two mythical amphibians belongs to Steve Conti. Photos of Sascha's beloved dog, Rocky, flank picture of Filomena Bruno.

Plate 504:
Sascha creations on corner walls of the dining room. The large cross is the original prototype for the 13' gold cross in St. Augustine Church in Santa Monica. This prototype now in the Dewayne Bethany collection.

Plate 505:
Collection of Daniel E. Fast,
M.D.

Plate 506:
Shower, main house.

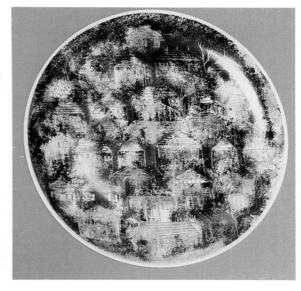

Plate 507:
Plates 507, 508, 509 from collection of Bill Seay.

Plate 508

Plate 509

Plate 510:
Obelisk, Lucite Egg.

Plate 511:
...more metal sculpture.

Plate 512:
Gold plated steel Rooster sculpture.

Plate 513:
Hortisculpture by Sascha, in
his own backyard.

🌾 *Vintage Photos* 🌾

When Sascha discovered how talented a photographer Bill Seay was, he "bought him all the equipment he could handle." The following shots were taken in the mid 1950s by Bill.

ABSTRACT

ABSTRACT

ABSTRACT

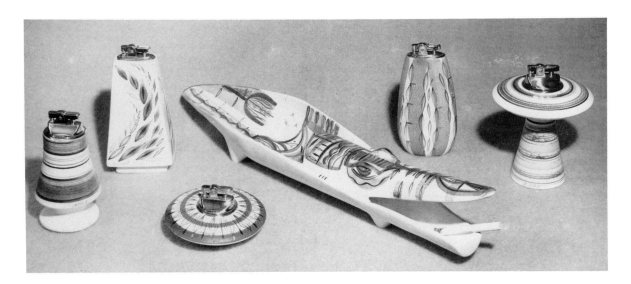

ABSTRACT

ABSTRACT

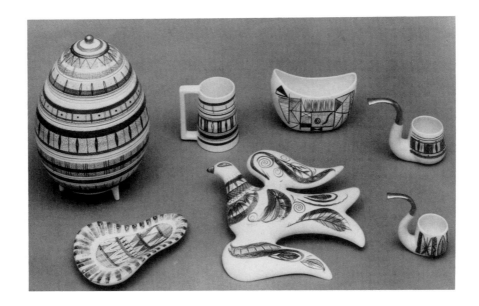

ABSTRACT

ABSTRACT

ABSTRACT

ABSTRACT

ALASKA

ALASKA

AMERICANA

AMERICANA

AMERICANA

AMERICANA

AMERICANA

ENAMEL

FIGURES
Black figures were modeled after some pre-Columbian original pieces
owned by Sascha.

FIGURES
Animals in black ceramic, Abstract design lighters and ashtray.

Ceramic bovine family.

LAMP BASES

MISCELLANEOUS LIGHTERS
Back in the '50s, cigarettes
were popular in every society.
These were essentials.

MOSAIC
Mosaic and raised designs.

MOSAIC
Various Mosaic masks. Lower left "Mayan," top 2 center panels
are African designs, on right is Alaskan "Walrus."

MOSAIC

MOSAIC

Original tile panel depicting "Lewis and Clark" theme.

Tile panel of Rooster.

Sascha original of sunflowers.

Egyptian style ceramic platter. Note Afghan dog lower left, modeled after one of Sascha's pets.

PERSIAN

RESIN OR RESOLITE

ROOFTOPS

SMOKE TREE
Tea canister.

Smoke Tree lamp bases.

VANITY FAIR

VANITY FAIR

❧ *Catalog Reprints* ❧

By the mid 1950s, Sascha was releasing two catalogs each year. The samples we've included were photographed by Bill Seay for the 1958 market. We've also added "press kit" information for retailers. Information is power...and we've given you plenty of it! Happy hunting!

Sascha Brastoff
PRODUCTS, INC.

DEAR CUSTOMER:

WE TAKE PLEASURE IN SENDING YOU OUR 1958 CATALOG, TOGETHER WITH PRICE LISTS AND ORDER BLANKS. YOU WILL FIND NEW PATTERNS, FORMS, AND TREATMENTS, EFFECTING GREATER CHANGES THAN USUAL IN OUR LINES. IN FACT, WE ARE SHOWING A LARGER NUMBER OF ENTIRELY NEW ITEMS THAN AT ANY TIME SINCE WE BEGAN BUSINESS.

THERE IS NO DOUBT AT ALL IN OUR MINDS THAT THE LINE AS NOW PRESENTED IS BY FAR THE MOST SALABLE EVER. WE ARE CONFIDENT YOU WILL AGREE WITH US.

YOU WILL ALSO FIND ENCLOSED A PRINT OF A FULL PAGE COLOR AD WHICH WILL APPEAR IN MAY HOUSE BEAUTIFUL, SUMMER BRIDES, AND MARCH I NEW YORKER. ADS OF SIMILAR COMPOSITION ARE APPEARING IN BLACK AND WHITE QUARTER PAGES IN THESE AND OTHER MAGAZINES THROUGH THE YEAR. WE LATER ON WILL MAIL YOU A COMPLETE SCHEDULE OF OUR 1958 NATIONAL ADVERTISING, AND IN AN EARLY SHIPMENT YOU WILL RECEIVE A COUNTER DISPLAY CARD FEATURING THE COLOR PAGE.

WE ANTICIPATE CONTINUING THE GOOD DELIVERY MAINTAINED THROUGH 1957, WHEN THE AVERAGE TIME BETWEEN ORDER AND SHIPMENT WAS LESS THAN 3 WEEKS. IN CASE YOU MAY BE UNABLE TO VISIT ONE OF OUR PERMANENT DISPLAYS, WE WOULD BE PLEASED TO SELECT AND SHIP TO YOU AN ASSORTMENT OF OUR NEW ITEMS, IN WHATEVER QUANTITY YOU WISH.

INASMUCH AS NATIONAL ADS FEATURING THESE NEW THINGS HAVE ALREADY APPEARED IN FEBRUARY HOUSE BEAUTIFUL AND SPRING BRIDES, MAY WE SUGGEST YOU TAKE ADVANTAGE OF THE RESULTING CONSUMER INTEREST WHILE STILL FRESH.

MAY WE TAKE THIS OPPORTUNITY OF THANKING YOU FOR YOUR PATRONAGE IN THE PAST, AND PARTICULARLY FOR YOUR HELP IN MAKING 1957 OUR MOST SUCCESSFUL YEAR TO DATE.

CORDIALLY,

SASCHA BRASTOFF PRODUCTS, INC.

E. E. Campbell

E. E. CAMPBELL, PRESIDENT

EEC/B

11520 WEST OLYMPIC BOULEVARD • WEST LOS ANGELES 64, CALIFORNIA

Sascha Brastoff

Sascha Brastoff's story is typically American. It could only happen here!

Born in 1920 in Cleveland, Ohio, he worked his way through The Cleveland School of Art, dressed windows at Macy's, danced with the Cleveland Ballet, and exhibited his sculptures at the Syracuse Museum, all before he was twenty. In the Air Force, he was a featured dancer in the great show, "Winged Victory," and after service he became a set and costume designer at 20th Century-Fox.

Ceramics was a hobby, and in 1947 he left the big studios, to set up shop in a little sheetiron building near his home in West Los Angeles. From this small beginning has grown the modern studio-factory which has become a must for tourists to Southern California, and from which his matchless signed originals go forth to fine shops and collectors in half a dozen countries.

When not designing for the market, supervising his art department, or making a personal appearance, he finds time to do original ceramic paintings and steel sculptures, which have found their way into the hands of numerous collectors and museums. In his current hobby, as a gold and jewelsmith, he creates for his friends fabulous rings, brooches, and cuff links, working in pure gold with the "lost wax" process.

This is similar to work done by de Vinci. One critic has termed Brastoff, "a sort of minor Leonardo," and not without good reason, as the mercurial versatility of his talent carries him with equal success thru one artistic field after another.

The boundless abilities of the man seem to culminate in and focus on his work in ceramic design. Certainly, in the world today he has no equal in this category, and the signature, "Sascha B.", stands as the hallmark of ceramic excellence.

COVER ILLUSTRATION:
Sun Rooster
Steel sculpture
by Sascha Brastoff
from the permanent
collection of the
Los Angeles County Museum.

Photography by Bill Sears

Free form clay sculpture
from gallery collection.

STUDIOS, GALLERIES AND TROPICAL GARDENS

Built in 1953, the Brastoff Ceramic Studios have been awarded the Certificate of Honor by the American Institute of Architects ... considered the nation's finest studio-factory designed to meet the exacting demands of highest quality pottery and fine china production. Their beautifully landscaped tropical gardens, with night time lighting effects, have received additional citations from design groups and the City Beautiful committee, Los Angeles Chamber of Commerce. Thousands of visitors annually are welcomed to these studios, to enjoy the exhibits and watch the artists at work.

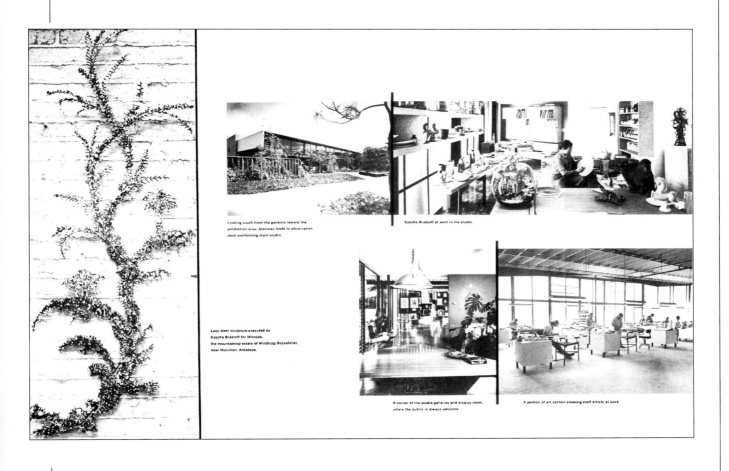

Looking south from the gardens toward the
production area. Stairway leads to observation
deck overlooking main studio.

Sascha Brastoff at work in his studio.

Lacy steel sculpture executed by
Sascha Brastoff for Winrock,
the mountaintop estate of Winthrop Rockefeller,
near Morrilton, Arkansas.

A corner of the studio galleries and display room,
where the public is always welcome.

A portion of art section showing staff artists at work.

CELADON

Pattern No. 24

A complete range of new designs . . .
hand-carved, gold-filled abstracts on
new foam textured Celadon glaze . . .
each piece a signed original.

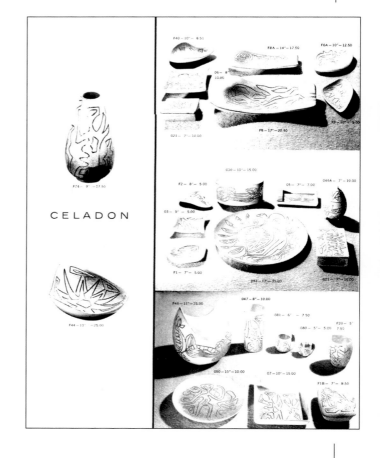

CELADON

ROOFTOPS

Pattern No. 10

A fresh rendition of one of Brastoff's most successful treatments . . . picturesque village impressions in high gloss. Magnificent colorings against a mist grey background highlighted in gold.

ROOFTOPS

044C — 13″ — 35.00

ABSTRACT ORIGINALS

Pattern No. 21

A fascinating and popular collection of original abstract designs in endless variety; soft pastel colors beneath a newly developed transparent and impervious matte glaze of velvet smoothness, accented with gold.

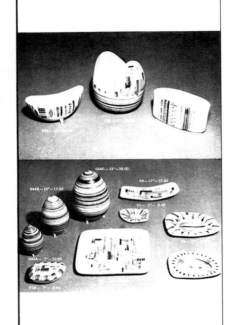

ABSTRACT ORIGINALS

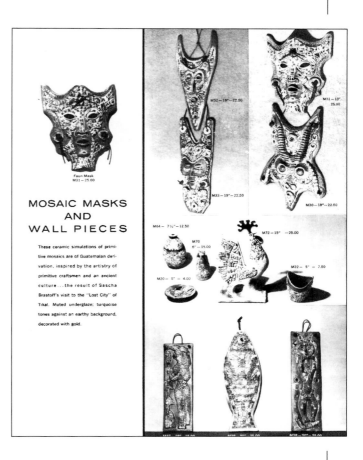

Faun Mask
M31 — 25.00

M32 — 19" — 22.50

M31 — 13"
25.00

MOSAIC MASKS
AND
WALL PIECES

These ceramic simulations of primitive mosaics are of Guatemalan derivation, inspired by the artistry of primitive craftsmen and an ancient culture...the result of Sascha Brastoff's visit to the "Lost City" of Tikal. Muted underglaze; turquoise tones against an earthy background, decorated with gold.

M33 — 19" — 22.50

M30 — 18" — 22.50

M64 — 7½" — 12.50

M70
6" — 15.00

M72 — 15" — 25.00

M20 — 5" — 4.00

M22 — 5" — 7.50

MS11 — 10" — 20.00

M O S A I C S
DECORATIVE
ACCESSORIES

M26 — 14" — 25.00

M66 — 6½ — 17.50

M5B — 9" Sq. — 17.50

M3 — 6" — 7.50

M69 — 9" — 17.50

M09 — 17" — 22.50

M10 — 17" — 37.50

M08 — 12" — 12.50

M8 — 11" — 17.50

M73 — 8" — 17.50

M4 — 13" — 25.00

M7 — 12" — 12.50

M5 — 8" — 12.50

MF6 — 12" — 20.00

M12 — 14" — 27.50

M9 — 12" — 12.50

M67 — 9" — 20.00

M2 — 7.50

M6 — 9" — 8.50

M14 — 17" — 25.00

ROMAN COIN — 5-pc. Place Setting 32.50

Innovations in an Ancient Art   FINE CHINA

Of heirloom quality, Brastoff fine china is original not only in pattern and in sculptural grace of design, but in the formulae for the medium itself. As a culmination of years of research, this china achieves the qualities toward which master potters have always aspired — amazing strength with light weight, and a superb translucence.

The patterns now in production were screened from more than 200 original Sascha Brastoff designs. For the first time, fine china is produced in a soft matte finish, combining the charm and informality of stoneware with the quality and elegance of porcelain. Designs are in the contemporary coupe shape. Created for the connoisseur, every piece is completely hand made.

ROMAN COIN

VANITY FAIR

ALLEGRO — 5-pc. Place Setting 25.50

JADE TREE — 5-pc. Place Setting 25.50

VANITY FAIR — 5-pc. Place Setting 25.50

FINE CHINA

ZEPHYR — 5-pc. Place Setting 27.50

LA JOLLA — 5-pc. Place Setting 30.00

WINROCK — 5-pc. Place Setting 30.00

CLASSIC — 5-pc. Place Setting 32.50

WINROCK

WINROCK

CUSTOM MADE DINNERWARE

Brastoff's custom made dinnerware has long been known for its excellent quality and high styling. His well known Surf Ballet patterns, acclaimed by decorators, offer something new and exciting in the field of table styling, complementary to any type of decor.

Moonfrost introduces a completely new feeling in earthenware. A blend of matte and high gloss achieves a frosty effect in its all-white center, and the texture of beaten metal in the broad border; available in both gold and silver.

MOONFROST — 5-pc. Place Setting 14.75

SURF BALLET — 5-pc. Place Setting 9.50

CP3 — 21"x 9" — 50.00

ORIGINAL CERAMIC PAINTINGS

An intriguing variety of original sub-
jects, hand-painted under glaze on
ceramic panels; beautifully framed,
ready for hanging.

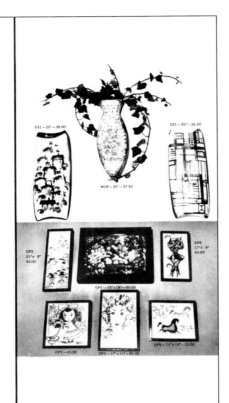

031 — 20" — 35.00

031 — 20" — 35.00

M29 — 20" — 37.50

CP3
21"x 9"
50.00

CP4
17"x 4"
40.00

CP1 — 23"x19" — 80.00

CP7 — 45.00

CP2 — 17"x 11" — 50.00

CP5 — 11"x 13" — 35.00

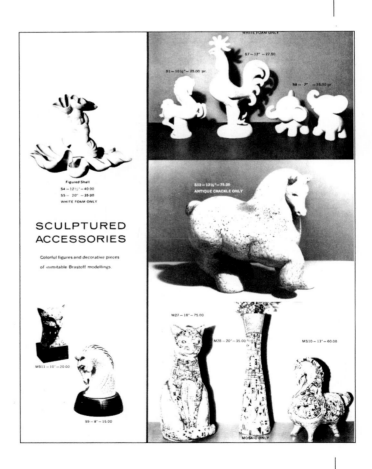

WHITE FOAM ONLY

S7 — 12" — 27.50

S1 — 10½" — 25.00 pr.

S8 — 7" — 25.00 pr.

Figured Shell
S4 — 12½" — 40.00
S5 — 20" — 35.00
WHITE FOAM ONLY

SCULPTURED ACCESSORIES

Colorful figures and decorative pieces
of inimitable Brastoff modellings.

S12 — 13½" — 75.00
ANTIQUE CRACKLE ONLY

MS11 — 10" — 20.00

M27 — 18" — 75.00

M28 — 20" — 35.00

MS10 — 13" — 60.00

S9 — 8" — 15.00

MOSAIC ONLY

LM-1 CARVED HORSE BLOCK 23" 120.00
Classic ancient horse block in bas-relief on earth-toned crackle glaze base. Matchstick shade in brown.

LM-4 MOSAIC EGG 27" 110.00
Carved simulated mosaic egg in tones of brown, gold and turquoise. Natural color matchstick shade banded in turquoise.

LM-7 ROOSTER 27" 105.00
Stylized rooster in brown crackle glaze with a proud gold crest. Brown and white matchstick woven shade.

CUSTOM MADE LAMPS

Sascha Brastoff's original lamp designs bring a fresh new approach to the field of home decoration . . . functional fine art, combining the world's leading style and quality in ceramics with the best in modern lighting. Hardwood bases, teak finish;

L-6A ABSTRACT EGG 27" 105.00
Bands of muted tones of blue, gold and brown on matte. White matchstick shade bordered with blue and brown.

L-23 ATHENA 35" 140.00
Startling white on white in abstract design blending to an all white matchstick shade.

L-29 TEMPLE DOG 36" 195.00
Antique crackled grey Chinese Guardian mounted on hand carved teak base. The shade is Celadon silk.

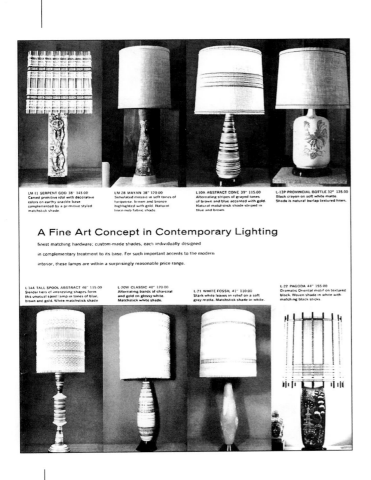

LM-11 SERPENT GOD 38" 145.00
Carved primitive idol with decorative colors on earthy crackle base complemented by a primitive styled matchstick shade.

LM-28 MAYAN 38" 120.00
Simulated mosaic in soft tones of turquoise, brown and bronze highlighted with gold. Natural linen nub fabric shade.

L-10A ABSTRACT CONE 39" 115.00
Alternating stripes of grayed tones of brown and blue accented with gold. Natural matchstick shade striped in blue and brown.

L-13P PROVINCIAL BOTTLE 32" 135.00
Black crayon on soft white matte. Shade is natural burlap textured linen.

A Fine Art Concept in Contemporary Lighting

finest matching hardware; custom-made shades, each individually designed in complementary treatment to its base. For such important accents to the modern interior, these lamps are within a surprisingly reasonable price range.

L-14A TALL SPOOL ABSTRACT 46" 115.00
Slender tiers of interesting shapes form this unusual spool lamp in tones of blue, brown and gold. White matchstick shade.

L-20W CLASSIC 40" 170.00
Alternating bands of charcoal and gold on glossy white. Matchstick white shade.

L-21 WHITE FOSSIL 41" 110.00
Stark white leaves in relief on a soft grey matte. Matchstick shade in white.

L-22 PAGODA 44" 155.00
Dramatic Oriental motif on textured black. Woven shade in white with matching black sticks.

L 24G BAL CAPRIE 39" 175.00
Venetian approach ... White foam and textured gold fluted vase. The shade is white shot with gold thread.

L 28F MINOS 40" 175.00
Textured matte figurines on silky white background. White textured silk shade bordered with gold.

L 31 SUNBURST 45" 150.00
Hand carved gold filled sunburst outlined on rough white. Shade: white silk, bordered with gold braid.

L 37 CAT GODDESS 18" 195.00
Egyptian weathered stone finish with carved detail. Shade: antique Celadon silk.

CUSTOM MADE LAMPS

L 33 SILVER TOWER 50" 185.00
Rough textured, beaten platinum accented with vertical cuttings. Shade: silver over white loose weave with beads accents.

L 34 COCTEAU 41" 160.00
The Eldorado of Lamps. Solid gold in rough texture with intaglio abstract carvings. Shade: gold and white accent jersey.

L 35 PINATA 45" 175.00
Abstract design in soft muted tones band the white matte base of this lamp with an unusual and interesting structural effect. Shade in woven white and gold.

L 36 VICTORIA 45" 160.00
The Gay 90's translated to Contemporary. Antique gold and black. The shade is silk jersey with gold threads.

BEHIND THE SCENES

A consummate craftsman, Brastoff employs every technique known to the ceramic industry, as well as some devised by and known only to himself. His ceramic productions present a marriage of chemistry and art, the result of painstaking effort on the part of his talented art staff, together with the most skillful handling and firing by his technicians. Achievement of the final effect necessitates, in almost every case, four overnight trips through the kilns. The result, a collector's item, bearing the famous signature, "Sascha B."

No two pieces are ever quite alike. The Brastoff artists follow a theme (but not a pattern) as set by Sascha himself, and each piece, being an original composition, must vary somewhat from every other. All the art work, with the exception of gold and silver touches, is done on the clay itself, and is sealed forever beneath an impervious coating of clear glaze. This is true even in the soft white matte glaze pieces, as this smooth satiny coating is also transparent. Gold and silver, due to their low melting points, must necessarily be applied over glaze. They are then fired into the glaze at lower temperatures.

Look for the signature— *SASCHA B.*

at America's most discriminating stores.

2. Finishing the casting

3. Applying the glaze spray

5. Loading kiln

4. A staff artist at work

6. Brastoff displays completed piece

PERMANENT EXHIBITS
Bolender & Co.
1951 Merchandise Mart
Chicago
Rees & Orr
225 Fifth Ave.
New York
Bill Jones
330 Santa Fe Building
Second Unit
Dallas, Texas
SASCHA BRASTOFF
PRODUCTS, INC.
11520 West Olympic Blvd.
West Los Angeles 64
California

ABSTRACT

ORIGINALS   *STOCK #21*

designed by SASCHA BRASTOFF

Abstract design depends for its charm and appeal upon a sensitive blending of colors, and upon an inspired concept in pattern and texture which harmonizes with its surroundings. Sascha Brastoff's interpretation of this motif has been a major artistic success.

The coloring and firing techniques which impart a unique "crackle" effect to the ABSTRACT Pattern were conceived and perfected by Sascha Brastoff. His versatility in all the media of sculpture and his mastery of ceramic art have won international recognition; but his artwares are primarily designed to add beauty to the home.

ABSTRACT ORIGINALS

appropriate with all concepts of home decor

as interpreted by

Sascha Brastoff

PRODUCTS, INC.

11520 W. Olympic Boulevard. Los Angeles 64

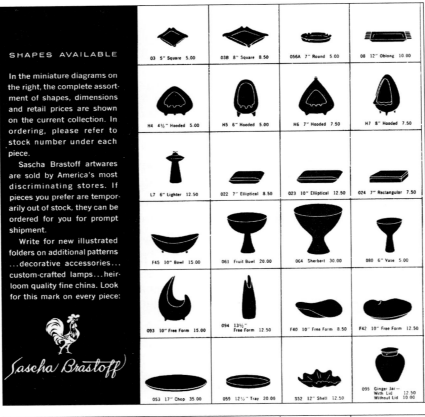

SHAPES AVAILABLE

In the miniature diagrams on the right, the complete assortment of shapes, dimensions and retail prices are shown on the current collection. In ordering, please refer to stock number under each piece.

Sascha Brastoff artwares are sold by America's most discriminating stores. If pieces you prefer are temporarily out of stock, they can be ordered for you for prompt shipment.

Write for new illustrated folders on additional patterns ...decorative accessories... custom-crafted lamps...heirloom quality fine china. Look for this mark on every piece:

Sascha Brastoff

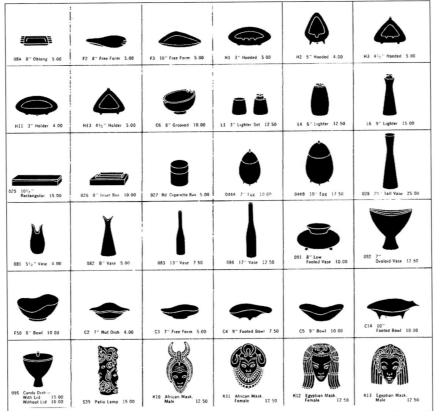

EXECUTIVE GIFTS

For the discriminating buyers of executive gifts, Sascha Brastoff provides the answer. In his inimitable way Sascha creates a customized gift recognized the world over for its outstanding quality.

There are many choices for the buyer. There are five beautiful patterns designed in sixty different shapes. Everyone of these hand decorated patterns represents a ceramic achievement never to be duplicated, for each one is an original.

There is also the possibility of personalized Sascha Brastoff gifts in any corporate image. Given a few facts on historical background, trade marks or industrial customs, Sascha will design an executive gift which typfies the giver. An executive gift designed by Sascha Brastoff will very subtly convey a personal message, never will it appear crass or commercial.

Several examples are shown in the photograph on the next page. On first inspection, these gifts appear to be regular decorative accessories. However, on closer inspection you will recognize such leading corporations as Sunkist, International Harvester, Haloid Xerox, Hawaiian Punch, United States Borax, Brown-Foreman, The Santa Monica Bank, as well as the state flag of Alaska.

We can individually design a gift for any corporation or event that will be a lasting memento. From past experience we know the vast majority of Sascha Brastoff gifts find their way to the recepient's home and in the home it is always sure to be a conversation piece. It is possible to apply a personal message on the back.

We will be very happy to discuss your gift needs in more detail at any time.

PRICE LIST - 1960
DECORATIVE ACCESSORIES
#21 Abstract Originals
#32 Midas
#33 Silver Wind
#34 Brocade
#35 Night Wind

ASHTRAYS

03	5" Square	5.00
03B	8" Square	8.50
056A	7" Round	5.00
08	12" Oblong	10.00
08A	8" Oblong	5.00
F2	8" Free Form	5.00
F3	10" Free Form	5.00
H1	3" Hooded	5.00
H2	5" Hooded	4.00
H3	4-1/2" Hooded	5.00
H4	4-1/2" Hooded	5.00
H5	6" Hooded	5.00
H6	7" Hooded	7.50
H7	8" Hooded	7.50
H11	3" Holder	4.00
H13	4-1/2" Holder	5.00
C6	8" Grooved	10.00

LIGHTERS

L1	3" Lighter Set	12.50
L4	6" Lighter	12.50
L6	9" Lighter	15.00
L7	6" Lighter	12.50

BOXES

022	7" Elliptical	8.50
023	10" Elliptical	12.50
024	7" Rectangular	7.50
025	10-1/2" "	15.00
026	8" Inset Box	10.00
027	Rd. Cig. Box	5.00
044A	7" Egg	10.00
044B	10" Egg	17.50

VASES - PLANTERS

028	20" Tall Vase	25.00
F45	10" Bowl	15.00
061	Fruit Bowl	20.00
064	Sherbert	30.00
080	6" Vase	5.00
081	5-1/2" Vase	4.00
082	8" Vase	5.00
083	13" Vase	7.50
084	17" Vase	12.50
091	8" Low Footed Vase	10.00
092	7" Ovaloid Vase	12.50
093	10" Free Form	15.00
094	13-1/2" Free Form	12.50

SERVERS

F40	10" Free Form	8.50
F42	10" Free Form	12.50
F50	8" Bowl	10.00
C2	7" Nut Dish	4.00
C3	7" Free Form	5.00
C4	9" Footed Bowl	7.50
C5	9" Bowl	10.00
C14	10" Footed Bowl	10.00
053	17" Chop	35.00
059	12-1/2" Tray	20.00

MISCELLANEOUS

S52	12" shell	12.50
095	Ginger Jar W/Lid	12.50
	Ginger Jar - No Lid	10.00
096	Candy Dish W/Lid	15.00
	Candy Dish - No Lid	10.00
S39	Patio Lamp	15.00
K10	Afr. Mask, Male	12.50
K11	Afr. Mask, Female	12.50
K12	Egp. Mask, Female	12.50
K13	Egp. Mask, Male	12.50

Sascha Brastoff Products, Inc., 11520 West Olympic Blvd., West Los Angeles 64, California

SUGGESTED ORDER - $200.00 (COST)

Stock No.	Description	Price	Quantity	Extension
03	5" Sq. Ashtray	$ 5.00	3	$ 15.00
03B	8" Sq. Ashtray	8.50	2	17.00
056A	7" Rd. Ashtray	5.00	4	20.00
08	12" Obl. Ashtray	10.00	1	10.00
08A	8" Obl. Ashtray	5.00	1	5.00
F2	8" Free Form	5.00	3	15.00
F3	10" Free Form	5.00	3	15.00
H1	3" Hooded Ashtray	5.00	2	10.00
H3	4-1/2" Hooded	5.00	3	15.00
H4	4-1/2" Hooded	5.00	1	5.00
H6	7" Hooded Ashtray	7.50	2	15.00
L1	3" Lighter Set	12.50	1	12.50
L6	9" Lighter	15.00	1	15.00
022	7" Elliptical Box	8.50	1	8.50
023	10" Elliptical Box	12.50	1	12.50
024	7" Rectangular Box	7.50	1	7.50
025	10-1/2" " "	15.00	1	15.00
027	Rd. Cigarette Box	5.00	2	10.00
044A	7" Egg	10.00	1	10.00
028	20" Tall Vase	25.00	1	25.00
080	6" Vase	5.00	1	5.00
082	8" Vase	5.00	1	5.00
091	8" Low Ftd. Vase	10.00	1	10.00
092	7" Ovaloid Vase	12.50	1	12.50
094	13-1/2" Free Form	12.50	1	12.50
F40	10" Free Form	8.50	2	17.00
F42	10" Free Form	12.50	2	25.00
C2	7" Nut Dish	4.00	2	8.00
C3	7" Free Form	5.00	2	10.00
C4	9" Ftd. Bowl	7.50	1	7.50
095	Ginger Jar	12.50	1	12.50
096	Candy Dish	15.00	1	15.00
			Total Retail	398.00
			Total Net	$199.00

SASCHA BRASTOFF PRODUCTS, INC.
11520 West Olympic Boulevard
West Los Angeles 64, California

SUGGESTED ORDER - $150.00 (COST)

Stock No.	Description	Price	Quantity	Extension
03	5" Sq. Ashtray	$ 5.00	2	$ 10.00
03B	8" Sq. Ashtray	8.50	1	8.50
056A	7" Rd. Ashtray	5.00	3	15.00
08	12" Obl. Ashtray	10.00	1	10.00
08A	8" Obl. Ashtray	5.00	1	5.00
F2	8" Free Form	5.00	2	10.00
F3	10" Free Form	5.00	2	10.00
H1	3" Hooded Ashtray	5.00	2	10.00
H3	4-1/2" Hooded	5.00	3	15.00
H4	4-1/2" Hooded	5.00	1	5.00
H6	7" Hooded Ashtray	7.50	2	15.00
L1	3" Lighter Set	12.50	1	12.50
L6	9" Lighter	15.00	1	15.00
022	7" Elliptical Box	8.50	1	8.50
023	10" Elliptical Box	12.50	1	12.50
024	7" Rectangular Box	7.50	1	7.50
027	Rd. Cigarette Box	5.00	2	10.00
044A	7" Egg	10.00	1	10.00
080	6" Vase	5.00	1	5.00
082	8" Vase	5.00	1	5.00
091	8" Low Ftd. Vase	10.00	1	10.00
092	7" Ovaloid Vase	12.50	1	12.50
094	13-1/2" Free Form	12.50	1	12.50
F40	10" Free Form	8.50	1	8.50
F42	10" Free Form	12.50	1	12.50
C2	7" Nut Dish	4.00	2	8.00
C3	7" Free Form	5.00	2	10.00
095	Ginger Jar	12.50	1	12.50
096	Candy Dish	15.00	1	15.00
			Total Retail	301.00
			Total Net	$150.50

SASCHA BRASTOFF PRODUCTS, INC.
11520 West Olympic Boulevard
West Los Angeles 64, California

Los Angeles Times   SUNDAY, NOV. 14, 1948—Part III 13

Poodle Plates

...by Sascha Brastoff...
inscribed with the name of your
poodle or theirs...one of so
many smart, amusing, original
gifts you will find in the Gift
Shop. For delivery by Christmas,
poodle plates must be ordered
before December 1.

Each **10.00**

Cannell & Chaffin
3000 WILSHIRE • IN WILSHIRE CENTER

FREE PARKING

Newspaper Ad – 1948

Ads from *House Beautiful, 1950s*

Ads from *House Beautiful, 1950s*

Ad slick circa 1950s

AS SEEN IN
House Beautiful THE NEW YORKER BRIDE'S

Sascha Brastoff

A man of many hands and many talents,
whose wizardry with clay, color,
form, and texture offers you breath-taking beauty
in articles of daily use.

CERAMIC ACCESSORIES — LAMPS — FINE CHINA —
each piece a signed original —
in America's finest stores.

SASCHA BRASTOFF PRODUCTS, INC., 11520 W. Olympic Blvd., Los Angeles 64 · Illustrated brochure, NY-4, 25¢

circa 1950s

Schroeder's
ANTIQUES
Price Guide

. . . is the #1 best-selling antiques & collectibles value guide on the market today, and here's why . . .

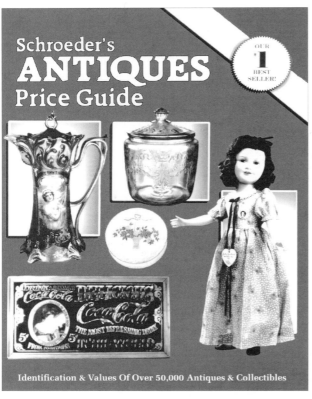

Schroeder's ANTIQUES Price Guide

OUR #1 BEST SELLER!

Identification & Values Of Over 50,000 Antiques & Collectibles

8½ x 11, 608 Pages, $12.95

• *More than 300 advisors, well-known dealers, and top-notch collectors work together with our editors to bring you accurate information regarding pricing and identification.*

• *More than 45,000 items in almost 500 categories are listed along with hundreds of sharp original photos that illustrate not only the rare and unusual, but the common, popular collectibles as well.*

• *Each large close-up shot shows important details clearly. Every subject is represented with histories and background information, a feature not found in any of our competitors' publications.*

• *Our editors keep abreast of newly developing trends, often adding several new categories a year as the need arises.*

If it merits the interest of today's collector, you'll find it in *Schroeder's*. And you can feel confident that the information we publish is up to date and accurate. Our advisors thoroughly check each category to spot inconsistencies, listings that may not be entirely reflective of market dealings, and lines too vague to be of merit. Only the best of the lot remains for publication.

Without doubt, you'll find
SCHROEDER'S ANTIQUES PRICE GUIDE
the only one to buy for
reliable information and values.

COLLECTOR BOOKS
A Division of Schroeder Publishing Co., Inc.